The Chivalry of Cheshire

Tony Bostock

First published in 1980 by E.J.Morten (Publishers), Manchester.

This ebook edition first published by Tony Bostock in 2016

EPUB ISBN 978-0-9956857-0-3

TONY BOSTOCK is an accomplished local historian. He holds a BA in History (Manchester, 1991) and an MA in Local History (Keele, 1994). He is the author of *Owners, Occupiers and Others; Seventeenth Century Northwich* and writes many articles on various aspects of Cheshire history, contributing regularly to the annual journal, *Cheshire History*. He was also editor and writer of the *Winsford Record* in the 1980s. Much of his work is published on his web-site: www.tonybostock.net. He is a regular speaker to local history and family history societies and other organisations such as Probus and W.I.s throughout the county, and has held posts as a part-time lecturer in these subjects.

As well as being a member of a number of academic societies in the region, he has been an active member of the Executive Committee of Cheshire Local History Association since its formation in 1998, and of its predecessor the Palatine Local History Committee. He chaired the Association for three, three-yearly terms and is now responsible for its website. He chaired Northwich Heritage Society and is currently treasurer of the Winsford Local History Society, of which he was also chairman for many years.

Having retired from a professional life in public service, Tony now applies himself more to the research and study of local and family history.

Table of Contents

PREFACE

This works starts in 1345, when the fifteen years-old Edward of Woodstock, Prince of Wales, Earl of Chester, known to history as the 'Black Prince', was embarking on his famous military career. It ends in 1399, at the conclusion of the reign of Richard II, the son of the 'Black Prince'. The period was that of Edward III, of Prince Edward and of King Richard; an age of war and peace; of sieges and tournaments of pillage and ransom; of colourful heraldry with emblazoned pennons, shields and surcoats. The time is often referred to as the Age of Chivalry, and hence the title. Some of Cheshire's sons became 'the flower of English Chivalry.'

When I wrote the first edition in 1980 I did not intend this work to be a scholarly history of England in the fourteenth century, or of her foreign policy, nor a detailed military history, likewise with this version. Rather, this is a study of the military activities of the Cheshire people linked to the major events of the period. Over three hundred Cheshire people are mentioned in the text and hundreds more are listed in the ten appendices. Any person with a Cheshire sounding surname should find an ancestor among the many names. Jonathan Sumption's excellent series on the Hundred Years War is a first-class study of the time for the student of English history.

Originally I extended thanks to the staff of various institutions and these ought to be recorded still: The Cheshire Record Office, The Public Record Office, The British Museum, Manchester Central Library, and the Macclesfield Library. I also thanked those who had read through the initial script and offered advice, and my then wife for her patience whilst I was busily engaged in typing the work and those thanks still stand. In addition I wish to add thanks to Anne and Jack Loader of Léonie Press for their advice in producing this e-book version.

Amazingly it has been 36 years since this book was first published. During that time much written about the Hundred Years Wars with France with new opinions. Also in that time computers have become part of everyday life and the internet has become an essential tool to gather and exchange information. As a result I decided to review the text and include some new information and also to edit some of the typographical errors which had unfortunately occurred in the original book. During the past several years e-books have become a very popular platform for publication and I therefore decided to launch this edition of *The Chivalry of Cheshire* in this modern format. Some maps have been added, the heraldic illustrations have been improved and I have also included some illustrations from the fourteenth century *Froissart's Chronicles*.

In some instances when direct quotations have been made from contemporary sources the passages have been modernised with regards spelling. The spelling of family names have been preserved in most cases.

I have to record my thanks to Martin Goldstraw for permission to copy his marvelous heraldic illustrations which he produced for the 'Cheshire Heraldry' web-site. In the original book the illustrations were black and white line drawings taken from Ormerod's *History of Cheshire*, but his coloured versions are a real bonus.

In essence the book is as it was originally, a tribute to those Cheshire men who served and fought for England and its kings in the latter half of the fourteenth century.

Tony Bostock
Swanlow
Winsford
2016

INTRODUCTION

The men of Cheshire chiefest for their place,
Of bone so big as only made for blows,
And have been ever fearful to their foes,
The northern men in feud so deadly fell.
That for their spear and horsemanship excel.
(Michael Drayton, *The Barons' Wars, Book 1*, 1596)

Because of Cheshire's continuity with Wales the county was considered to be an area of military importance. During the eleventh, twelfth and thirteenth centuries Wales was a hostile country ruled over by its Gaelic princes and the fierce Welshmen constantly raided the English borderlands. Cheshire, a strategic base and a constant source of manpower, was not considered a part of England but a separate area ruled over by its earl. The county had its own customs and laws, its people were not represented in Parliament and they did not pay national taxes. The first Norman earl, in the time of William the Conqueror, was Hugh d'Avaranches, a nephew of the king. Earl Hugh and his descendants enjoyed regal status in the Cheshire until the death of John le Scot, the seventh and last independent Earl of Chester. Cheshire's independence was such that when Magna Carta was sealed in 1215 by King John its provisions were not applicable in Cheshire, so the county had its own charter issued by the earl. In 1231 the earldom became vested in the crown as an endowment of the eldest son of the sovereign, but the people of the county still retained their ancient customs, laws and privileges.

The burden placed on the County in defending the Welsh marches (borderlands) was very heavy and consequently the men of Cheshire were excused military duties elsewhere in the realm. When no danger threatened Cheshire men were excused duty as castle-guard at Chester and the earl was able to call on men from his English estates to perform this chore. When danger threatened the feudal host of Cheshire was summoned. Earl Ranulph, the sixth earl, in his great charter of 1215 stated:

Each of the barons, when need arises in war shall fully perform the services of as many knight's fees as he holds, and their knights and free tenants shall have breastplates and haubergeons and may defend their fees with their bodies even if they are not knights; and if any such be unable so to defend his land he may find a substitute.

The term 'knight's fee' in the charter means a portion of land held by a man in return for military service to his lord. The Earl would therefore expect his barons to perform military duty dependent upon the amount of land they held. Similarly the baron would expect the same of his knights and sub-tenants.

Due to the county's low population the men of Cheshire were unable to evade their responsibilities by paying 'scutage' (a fine) as the knights of England could: if a Cheshire man could not perform his duty he had to find a substitute. Any lack of manpower was overcome to some degree by a system of 'advowry'. The city and county of Chester had always been considered a place of refuge for an English outlaw where he could be beyond the reach of English law. Such a person could call upon a baron of the county and request 'advow' (protection) and be granted it subject to him performing military service for the earl. Rudheath, Overmarsh and Hoole Heath were distinct places in the county set aside for the renegade Englishmen to settle. The immigrant lawless Englishmen helped to create the bad reputation the county was to receive from the historians of the time - a place of lawlessness and violence.

* * *

Because of the Cheshire men's experience at fighting the Welsh the numbers sent on the campaigns in north and central Wales were disproportionately high in comparison with other counties of the kingdom. Early in the reign of Edward I a force of 1,000 Cheshire men, comprising archers and foot soldiers, formed part of an army of 2,576 raised by the sovereign for service in Wales. In addition a special squad of one hundred archers from Macclesfield served throughout the campaign at 3*d* a day. By comparison the counties of Shropshire and Stafford provided 640 men, Lancashire 120, leaving little over 700 to be raised elsewhere. Later in the same year, 1217, about 620 men from Cheshire went into North Wales as reinforcements. In January 1283, an army 5,000 strong served in Wales of whom 2,000 were Cheshire men.

The men of Cheshire could not be compelled to serve in South Wales but in 1287 a special request was made and consequently several hundred assisted in quelling a rebellion there. In the Welsh rebellions of 1295 the county had 1,300 men serving in North Wales. In 1297 Cheshire men journeyed to Scotland: 4,000 men were requested but only about three-quarters of the number are thought to have gone on the journey north. In the following year 1,000 Cheshire men formed the King's guard, amongst an army of 12,000 who saw action at the battles of Stirling Bridge and Falkirk. In 1308, Cheshire sent 400 men to Scotland, as compared with Stafford's 300 and Shropshire's 200 and in 1322, one thousand were arrayed for service in the north.

The Cheshire men filled all the various ranks of the medieval army from man-at-arms of the knightly class to common foot soldier, but the greatest numbers were employed as archers. '*Old Cheshire is well known to be the Chief of Men*' wrote the seventeenth century poet Michael Drayton and of these the archer must surely rank supreme, for it was his accuracy with the longbow which helped make England victorious over the French. Many scions of the knightly families had learnt the skill of the longbow from the Welsh mountain men and eventually surpassed them in its use - the Cheshire archer of Edward III's day ranking superior to his Welsh counterpart. The tactics which were to prove so successful in France were forged at the battles of Falkirk in 1298 and Homildon Hill in 1333. A combination of men-at-arms and archers was used, with the latter tightly packed in a wedge formation at the end of each division of men-at-arms, thus producing a deadly cross-fire situation for the advancing enemy - a 'harrow' formation.

* * *

The men-at-arms were the knights and esquires of the county. A knight could be either a banneret or a bachelor: the former being the more senior. A knight bachelor was a knight of 'a single shield' - one who held no responsibility for other knights and was not sufficiently wealthy to retain other knights: he went to war without a retinue other than a servant or two. A bachelor followed in the service of a banneret, who was a commander with a retinue of bachelors, esquires and foot soldiers. A knight bachelor could be promoted to the rank of banneret on gaining sufficient monetary rewards to own sufficient lands to retain other knights, and having proved himself on the field of battle. A knight bachelor carried a long triangular pennon on which his arms were displayed; if promoted on the field of battle his commander would slice the tail of the pennon off, creating a square banner, hence banneret. A bachelor could be delegated a position of command: he could for example be given responsibility of a contingent of archers in his lord's retinue. An esquire could be promoted to the rank of knight bachelor on proving himself worthy financially and militarily - some, however, were unwilling to take on the burden of knighthood.

During the thirteenth century the recruitment of an army underwent change. The old idea was based on the obligation of holding lands from a lord but towards the end of the century, and at the start of the fourteenth, a system of issuing indentures to professional troops began. The old 'feudal system' was inefficient as it required service for only forty days a year and most of those who served were hardly willing. Edward began to issue indentures to 'regular' soldiers which meant he would be served by a body of professional soldiers, hardened campaigners, men who would willingly serve for as long as necessary at set rates of pay. The contract between sovereign and the local leader would stipulate how many men he was to have in his retinue and for how long they were to serve. The local leader in a county might then rely on the feudal system to recruit his retinue or make out indentures with those willing to serve him. The men of Cheshire were mainly recruited through the old system; the king would issue an indenture with his son, as Earl of Chester, who would then issue instructions to his administrators to array the men of Cheshire who owed him service. In addition to Cheshire, the Earl of Chester, also recruited men from his vast estates in his principality of Wales and his estates in the Duchy of Cornwall, but it was his Cheshire men who received the highest wages and the better positions in his army. Other magnates in England having holdings in Cheshire might also recruit men from their estates, but the Prince had prior claim to the men of the county.

The following provide good examples of indentures, though not necessarily involving Cheshire men. The Earl of Northampton was contracted to provide two bannerets, 46 knights, 112 men-at-arms, and 141 archers, in 1346; the Earl of Salisbury was contracted to provide six knights, 20 men-at-arms, and 24 archers, at a total rate of £76 pounds for every forty days: Lord Talbot - 157 men of whom 82 were archers; and at the bottom of the scale, Sir Walter de la Pole, was indentured to provide two men-at-arms and two archers.

Although this work begins in 1345 the Cheshire men-at-arms and archers had seen service in France at an earlier date. In 1340, four thousand men-at-arms and 12,000 archers fought a sea battle off Sluys, a Flemish harbour; the French were sitting ducks to the English archers' rapid fire and many of these archers were Cheshire men. In September 1342 the first pitched land battle of the Hundred Years Wars was fought at Morlaix in Brittany. The Earl of Northampton with an army of 3,000, of whom the majority were archers, besieged the town of Morlaix. When a relieving army of 15,000 men under Charles de Blois appeared on the scene, the Earl realised he would have to give battle and selected a suitable site on an area of sloping ground. He placed his army near the top of the slope with their backs to a copse: a trench was dug 50 yards in front of their position. The men were then formed up into a harrow formation. A strong line of dismounted men was the sight which presented itself to Charles de Blois. The French, who nearly always fought on horseback, charged the line. Each time the French charged they were beaten back by the accuracy of the English archers. Those who got through the early stages of the charge fell foul of the trench and the nearer they got to the English lines the fiercer the cross-fire. The French cavalry were thrown into confusion, and after the third charge they completely withdrew, leaving the English victorious.

This was the first major victory of the wars to come and gave England a taste for further victory. Her small, well disciplined army had defeated a far superior force of French cavalry, with few casualties. England's recipe of men-at-arms and archers in a harrow formation was to be repeated time and time again.

* * *

The fourteenth century was a period of change in the style of armour worn by the men-at-arms. It was a time of transition from mail to plate armour; as the century progressed, the emphasis on plate armour increased. It must not be assumed that any particular fashion was universal at any particular moment, as many styles would have been evident depending on its wearer's fancy or on his financial and professional status. Those who saw little military service were content to retain their old fashioned chain mail amour, others, with greater need equipped themselves with the modern styles.

The previous style of body armour comprised of padded garments and mail, with the possible addition of plate at the shoulders, elbows and knees', instead of plate a poorer man might wear *cuir boulli*, a form of hardened leather. Over the layers of padding the warrior wore a surcoat, often knee length, on which his heraldic device was displayed, hence 'coat of arms'. The head was protected by a tight padded cap covered by mail, over this a round topped helmet of steel may have been worn. The newer variety of armour had curved steel plates to protect the limbs, and buckled on the inside of the limb. To protect the inside of the joints - the elbows, shoulders and knees - special fan shaped pieces were added. The feet were encased in strips of steel, each plate overlapping another in a lobster tail fashion. The gauntlets were constructed in a similar fashion. The chest and back were protected by shaped steel plates; the breast plate produced a very distinctive globular shape. From the breast and back plates there hung a skirt of mail reaching to mid thigh, to protect the loins. Gussets of mail appeared at various vulnerable places the inside of the elbow, armpit and the rear of the knee. Chain mail was also used to protect the shoulders and neck and was fashioned into a cape which swept down from the base of the helmet to the edge of the shoulders. The *camail* or *aventail* as it is sometimes known, is a particular feature of armour of the period: it was fastened to the helmet by means of a leather thong threaded through staples which are sometimes to be seen on effigies covered by a decorative border. The steel plates worn by the men-at-arms were probably painted to protect them from rusting and to avoid glare when hidden to prevent the wearer from being detected. Armour might be coloured, to suit the wearer, or to suit his family's livery colour. In Malory's *Idylls of King Arthur*, knights of various colours are mentioned. Green is suggested in the fourteenth century poem, *Sir Gawain and the Green Knight*. This poem gives a clear indication as to how the medieval warrior armed himself. Incidentally the poem speaks of its hero travelling to the Wirral in mid-winter. The authorship of the poem is uncertain but it is generally credited to Hugh Mascy of Potington, on the Wirral.

The helmet, *bacinet*, was originally round topped without sides to protect the ears. As time progressed the crown was developed into a point, and the back and sides extended downwards. Some warriors covered their faces with a visor, which had a distinctive pointed snout. The long 'coat of arms' was shortened to produce a close-fitting, thigh-length garment known as a *jupon*. It consisted of a number of layers of coarse material covered then with silk or velvet, onto which the wearer's 'arms' were embroidered or painted. A feature of this style of armour, or 'harness' as it was often then referred to, was the broad hip belt from which the sword and dagger were hung. The belt, *baldric*, was often richly fashioned with round or oblong brooches studded with jewels. No doubt the richer the man, the more elaborate the belt: it is often referred to as the 'knightly belt". It is a common mistake to consider the armoured man-at-arms a slow moving person who needed help to mount a horse and helpless if thrown to the ground. Contemporary accounts often refer to men-at-arms being thrown to the ground, picking themselves up and fighting on foot. The weight of the armour worn during the latter half of the century was perhaps of a similar weight to the ceremonial uniform worn by the Household Cavalry today.

A man-at-arms was equipped with a sword with a blade designed for stabbing and slashing. Its hilt had a straight, or slightly down curving, cross guard, and a round pommel. A second sword with a longer, thinner blade may have been carried at the saddle and used for thrusting, much in the way that a lance would be used. A lance was carried by some mounted infantrymen who were known as a 'hobelars'. The dagger, *misericorde*, hung at the hip from the belt, had a straight trangular blade and was used to give the final 'mercy' blow to a fallen adversary. A man-at-arms may have carried a pole-axe (its name describes it perfectly) with a shaft of about five feet in length and having a blade on one side for cutting and a spike on the other for piercing armour: it is believed that it was a popular weapon among the ordinary man-at-arms. Clubs and maces of various designs were also used - one of the most common had a spiked ball at the head of a four foot shaft and another was the war hammer, much like a large size claw hammer of today. A shield was carried by men-at-arms in the early days of the century but as the use of plate increased, its use decreased. Men-at-arms continued to use the shield in the tournament, but rarely in battle.

* * *

The man-at-arms' humbler comrade, the archer, was attired in a light weight fashion. Over his body he wore a leather jerkin, under which he had a padded jacket. In some case the jerkin was reinforced with metal plates or studs – a*brigandine*: those who could afford it wore a small breast plate of steel. On his left arm the archer wore a leather bracer to prevent the bowstring from chaffing the inside of the forearm. His limbs were relatively unprotected. On his head he wore a simple steel cap. Archers might serve on foot or mounted.

The archer's weapon was of course the longbow made from yew, ash or elm; the finest wood being the yew. Laws were passed making it compulsory for every village to plant and preserve yew trees and accordingly yew trees are often found in Cheshire church yards. The bow would measure between five and six feet in length and would require a pull of between sixty and ninety pounds. In cross section the weapon was 'D' shaped, with the flat surface facing the target. It was made from a single piece of wood with notches carved at top and bottom to retain the loops of the bowstring. The bow strings were made from good flax or linen and were impregnated with bee's wax to protect them from the weather. The arrow measured between thirty and thirty-six inches long, barbed with iron and fledged with goose or peacock feathers. The archer normally carried a sheaf of twenty-four arrows at his belt and have others issued to him from the baggage train. He would place the arrows in the ground in front of him before a battle to enable him to fire at a fast rate. An archer could shoot six arrows a minute and be very accurate; no doubt he could be faster if he shot a general volley into the air without aiming. The whole of the archer's body was employed in drawing the bow, not just the arm; he would lean himself back to draw. The effective range appears to have been about a furlong (220 yards). There have been records of greater distances but these are probably no more than legend. Shakespeare, in Henry IV, part II, speaks of the prowess of an old archer, and puts the following words into the mouth of Justice Shallow.

...he drew a good bow
.....he shot a fine shoot;
John o' Gaunt loved him well
and betted much money on his head..
He could have clapped in the clout at twelve score,
and carried you a forehand shaft a fourteen and
fourteen and a half,
that it would have done a man's heart good to see... .

Shakespeare then is giving the bowman an accurate range of 240 yards, and a range of 290 yards with an arrow aimed at a height no higher than the eye. An arrow aimed with a slight elevation went further, but with less accuracy.

An archer also carried a sword and a dagger. The sword issued to the archer differed slightly from the type used by the men-at-arms by being fashioned to produce a cutting stroke and was therefore broader and heavier. In the later years of the century the humble warrior carried a 'falchion', a type of sword with a broad curved blade shaped to produce a convex cutting edge with greater width at its bottom end, thus creating extra weight to the cutting stroke. A finger guard was attached to the pommel: essential to protect his fingers. Captured archers invariably had their first two fingers of the right hand amputated in case they should escape to use the bow again. It is thought that today's 'two fingered salute' – the 'V' sign – originated at this time as an act of defiance shown to an advancing foe.

The English archer, although of humble origins as compared to the man-at- arms and knight, was to reign supreme from 1340 onwards; of them the Cheshire bowmen were given the place of honour, and rank supreme. Hedley Lucas, a twentieth century poet, writes:

Cheshire men who drew,
The English bowmen's way
Cheshire men who's arrows flew,
As sure as sunshot speeds the day.

Feared on a foreign field,
Famed on their native ground,
Foes who would never yield,
All seasoned in the round.

Gone is those archers might,
A whistling deadly storm,
Yet in a fancy's flight,
See ghostly ranks reform.

At Crecy, Agincourt and Poitiers,
As guard of Richard II's life,
The backbone of his sway,

And in the Rose's strife,
Cheshire men who broke the lines
Of many a doughty foe,
Whose laurelled valour shines,
Whenever bends the bow.

1. CAEN, CRÉCY AND CALAIS

It was June 1345 and England had been at peace with France since the signing of the Treaty of Malestroit in January 1343. The truce had been declared at the end of six years of Anglo-French hostilities following Edward III's inconclusive expedition to Brittany in support of John de Monfort's claim to that duchy. By the terms of the agreement each side was to keep what they held: the Monfort faction and England to retain the south and west of the duchy whilst de Blois and France the north and east. The rivalry had occurred after the death of the old duke of Brittany in 1342, for according to 'salic' law the Duchy should have been inherited by the older duke's brother John de Montfort whilst de Blois believed he had a better right, having married one of the old Duke's heiresses. As heir also to the English Earldom of Richmond, de Montfort sought and received King Edward's support.

Before the end of 1344 the conditions of the treaty were broken. King Philip VI of France, in support of de Blois' claim to the whole duchy, had de Montfort's supporters put to death. John de Montfort fled to England and appealed to King Edward, who perhaps needed little excuse to renew hostilities, and once again proclaim himself King of France.

Edward decided upon a three-pronged attack on France: from the south through his Duchy of Aquitaine; from the west through Brittany, and from the north through Flanders. Henry Grosmont, Earl of Derby, was appointed lieutenant of Acquitaine and despatched to south-west France. Henry, at forty-five, was a seasoned campaigner as he had fought in all the French campaigns and crusaded against the Moors in Prussia and Granada. The second prong was led by William de Bohun, Earl of Northampton, the Constable of England, who has seen previous service with Derby in Brittany. The final stage of the offensive was undertaken by Edward who sailed to Flanders to win support through negotiations with Jacob van Artevelde, a wealthy merchant of Ghent. However, during the negotiations Artevelde was murdered and nothing came of the visit. Disappointed, Edward returned home.

Derby landed at Bayonne in June 1345 with a force of 2,000 consisting of nearly equal numbers of men-at-arms, mounted archers, foot archers, and Welsh spearmen. From Bayonne the army marched to Bordeaux and Liboume where King Edward's second cousin was well received by the people of the duchy, who had been loyal to the English crown and continually fought off French encroachments. Under Derby's banner many Cheshire men marched. The house of Lancaster, of which Derby was son and heir, owned estates in Cheshire and many of his tenants would have followed him. In the same army, Sir Ralph de Stafford, later Earl of Stafford, as keeper of the estates of the young Prince of Wales, Earl of Chester, would have led many Cheshire men under his banner.

Derby's first successes were in taking the town of Bergerac in the month of August and the whole of the province of Agenais in the following month. From there he moved into Périgord, established a garrison at Auberoche, nine miles from the provincial capital of Périgueux, and then returned to Bordeaux all within two months of his landing in France. The French retaliated by laying siege to Auberoche, using several thousand men. In response Derby sent 400 men-at-arms and 800 archers to relieve the outpost and the Earl of Pembroke was ordered to gather a force and to march in support. After a rapid march Derby and his force camped in a wood near to the town and waited for Pembroke. As the reinforcements failed to arrive Derby decided to attack the French besiegers and caught them off-guard as they were cooking and eating their evening meal. After an initial volley of arrows the men-at-arms charged out of the woods and a fierce hand-to-hand battle took place. As the French were beginning to gain the upper-hand, the pro-English garrison sallied out and took the French from behind. By nightfall the battle was over, the French commander and his lieutenants were prisoners, and each English man-at-arms had two or three prisoners worthy of ransom. Having failed to reach Auberoche in time Stafford and his retinue fell south to take the town of Aiguillon on the River Garonne some thirty miles above La Réole.

Following his success at Auberoche Derby headed home to Bordeaux by way of La Réole which he besieged for ten weeks before; its garrison surrendered having been deceived into thinking that its walls had been mined. In four months Derby, Stafford and Manny had taken the whole of two provinces, secured them against the French and garrisoned nearly fifty castles. During this campaign Henry heard of his father's death and that he had therefore inherited the vast estates of the duchy of Lancaster. Unlike Derby and his lieutenants, John de Montfort, with the Earl of Northampton and Sir

Thomas Dagworth, scored little success during 1345 and were ordered back to England to await the Spring.

* * *

Throughout the winter months Edward prepared for a large scale invasion of France by gathering finances and recruiting men. He issued indentures to local leaders in every county south of the Trent; those to the north were kept for action against England's other arch-enemy, Scotland. The rates of pay were high: an earl received 6s 8d a day, a banneret 4s, a bachelor 2s, a man-at-arms 1s, a mounted archer and the Cheshire archers 6d, and the subordinate archers and foot soldiers various payments down to 2d a day. Every man from the Prince of Wales to common soldier received the king's wages.

In Cheshire archers were raised by means of Commissions of Array issued to the Justiciar of Chester, Sir Thomas de Ferrers, or his lieutenant Roger de Hopwood. The orders stated a number of men should be chosen, tested and arrayed for service; the order invariably indicated where they were to assemble, and by what date. Orders were issued to the Chamberlain of Chester, Master John de Burnham, the younger, requiring him to supply cloth for coats and hats to those arrayed. The coats and hats were to be of wool, coloured green and white, divided vertically, green to the right of each item. The uniform was only issued to the archers from Cheshire and Flint (a county in the Principality of Wales which was then administered from Chester) and these uniforms appear to be the first uniform worn by an English army. The Chamberlain was also given instructions as to the payments these men were to receive. Archers from South and North Wales were also recruited in the same fashion but there is no record of them being issued with a distinctive uniform.

King Edward planned to start his invasion in February 1346 and ordered that ships be ready by Candlemas (2 February). That month the plans were put off until Easter and during that time orders were issued to the young Prince Edward to array 3,550 of his subjects in Wales, half of whom were to be archers and the other half spearmen. During Lent the invasion was again put off because of stormy weather, then on 30 April King Edward issued further orders to his son:

> *...to array without fail those three thousand five hundred and fifty Welshmen who were ordered to be arrayed in Wales and those one hundred archers who were ordered to be arrayed in*

the county of Chester and armed with bows, arrows, lances and other suitable arms and to cause them to be brought to Portsmouth at the Quindene of Easter.

The Earl of Northampton, Dagworth and de Montfort had left for Brittany in the Spring and scored a success in taking the town of La Roche-Derrien. They then made a *chevauchée* (a fast cavalry raid made with the intention of inflicting severe damage upon enemy territory) across the duchy, culminating in a victory at St. Pol de Léon on 9 June, where Dagworth's archers shot their way out of a very difficult position and defeated a superior French army. A little later, in a battle near La Roche-Derrien, Charles de Blois was taken prisoner and sent under escort to London. Hugh Calveley, Robert Knolles and Walter Hewitt, three Cheshire squires, served in the retinue of Sir Thomas Dagworth and are believed to have been present at both Pol de Léon and Roche-Derrien. Much more will be heard of Calveley and Knolles later.

Edward's main expedition was put off again until mid-summer. On 20 June Sir Hugh Hastings, son of the Earl of Pembroke, was appointed the king's lieutenant in Flanders and was sent to the Low Countries to rally support for an invasion from the northern border of France. During June and July, the English army assembled on the Hampshire coast and on Saturday, 8 July, orders were issued by the prince to Roger de Hopwell:

...if he has not yet fully carried out the prince's late order to him to choose, make trial of and array, three hundred archers in the county of Cestre and Flynt, and furnish them with bows, arrows and other arms so as to be ready at the prince 's call to make trial of and array the said archers with all speed, and appoint for each hundred of them a man-at to be their leader, so that they be ready and apparelled by Wednesday or Thursday at the latest. He is not to go out of his bailiwick until the archers be delivered to those whom the prince shall send for them, and is to arrest all whom he shall find rebellious or contrariant, and keep them in the castle (at Cestre) without bail or mainprise until further order.

A similar charge was sent to the lieutenant of the Justice of North Wales. The next month an order was sent to the Chamberlain:

In pursuance of an order to Roger de Hopwell... to send to the prince one hundred of the best of the three hundred archers of the counties of Cestre and Flint, whose array was lately ordered so that they be at Sandewiz on Sunday after the Assumption [15 August] to pay the said archers six pence a day each for their wages from the time of their departure out of the county of Cestre until their arrival at Sandewiz, and to have them clothed as the other archers with the prince were clothed, and pay Sir William de Brereton their leader two shillings a day. Great care is to be taken that they are the best of the three hundred archers, and that they be charged to make as long marches as possible, for the day of passage is soon.

The expeditionary force numbered around 15,000. The sixteen years old Prince had a personal retinue of eleven bannerets, 102 bachelors, 264 men-at-arms, 384 mounted archers, with a further 582 others: of the total of 1,343, about 500 were Welsh, and another 500 were Cheshire men. Amongst the men-at-arms in the Prince's retinue were Sir John Hyde of Hyde who served with a Thomas Crue and his brother, and Sir Thomas Daniers of Bradley. Also in the retinue was Sir James d'Audley of Helegh, a Staffordshire knight who held large estates in southern Cheshire.

On Southsea Common the army assembled: from king to humble yeoman, from professional knight in search of bounty to common criminal in search of a pardon. Not all were combatants as there were carpenters, miners, grooms, and armourers; smiths, cooks and vintners; priests, doctors and heralds. All speculated on their destination: was it to be Brittany in support of the Constable? Flanders to follow Hastings? Or Aquitaine to help Lancaster who was then at La Réole, helpless to relieve the siege of Aiguillon where Pembroke and Manny were desperately holding out against the Dauphin's large army?

On 11 July, the expedition set sail for Normandy thus opening up a fourth front to keep the French occupied and to draw her great army away from Aquitaine. The following day the army began to disembark on the Cotentin peninsula at St. Vaast la Hogue. They camped for nearly a week whilst troops and supplies were unloaded: ships journeying back and too with their cargoes. During the morning of Monday, 17 July, 1346, the army, led by the vanguard under its nominal head the Prince of Wales, set off into France. Ahead of the main body rode a Norman exile, Geoffrey de Harcourt, lord of Saint Saveur le Vicomte, who had been exiled for his attempt to seize the duchy of Normandy from King Philip's son, John. It was

Harcourt who advised Edward to land in Normandy as it was virtually undefended. His troop rode some fifteen miles in advance returning every two or three days with intelligence, plunder, and provisions. The Earl of Warwick did likewise but keeping to the seaward side of the main army. The Earl of Huntingdon commanded several vessels of the fleet and followed the invasion along the Norman coast, raiding and burning the ports whilst providing a moveable base and reserve force.

From their landing place the army moved to Valognes, then Carenton and by Saturday arrived at St. Lô, having taken many places by force on the way. By way of Calvados they marched on to Caen, the richest town in the province, which they reached on the 25 July. Edward arranged his army in a semi-circle around the north of the town, and camped for the night. The Prince's division lodged at the Abbaye aux Dames on the eastern side of the town. Inside the town the chivalry of northern France were assembled with the Marshal, Chamberlain and Constable of France.

Caen was situated at the confluence of two rivers: the Orne which flows to the sea at Ouistreham, where the English fleet lay at anchor, and the Odon. The town was split into two separated by the Odon which created a defence for the newer part of the town. The people of Caen and its defenders occupied this new part as it was virtually an island with the bridges leading to it heavily guarded. The fight to take the town was a hard one but the skill of the English archers overcame that of the French cross-bowmen and, with the support of the fleet which sailed down the River Orne, the town was taken within a day. This was followed by much slaughter and as many as 5,000 are said to have perished.

> *... Meanwhile the English men-at-arms, and archers were continuing the slaughter of the fugitives, sparing none. Looking out from the gate tower where they were taking refuge, and seeing the truly terrible carnage which was taking place in the street the Constable and the Count began to fear that they themselves would be drawn into it and fall into the hands of the archers who did not know them. While they were watching the massacre in dismay, they caught sight of a gallant English knight with only one eye called Sir Thomas Holland, and five or six other knights with him. They recognised him because they had campaigned together in Granada and Prassia and other expeditions, in the way in which knights do meet each other. They were much relieved*

when they saw him and called out to him as he passed, 'Sir Thomas come and speak to us... come to us in this gate house and make us your prisoners...

Sir Thomas was delighted at the prospect of such valuable prisoners. He took sixteen men up to the tower and claimed the prisoners for himself and his fellow knights then, leaving men to guard them, he continued through the town. Sir Thomas Holland of Holland in South Lancashire, eventually sold his prisoner, the Count of Eu, Constable of France, to the king for the considerable sum of 80,000 florins (about £12,000). Holland was not actually blind in one eye, but had vowed, as had 40 other young bachelors at the start of the French wars, to keep an eye covered until he had performed some deed of valour in France. His sister Joan, married Sir Hugh Dutton of Dutton, a Cheshire knight. The passage from Froissart's *Chronicles* relates to other knights one of whom was Sir Thomas Daniers of Bradley, a Cheshire man, who had as his prisoner the Chamberlain of France, the Lord Tankerville. The Prince of Wales, as Earl of Chester and therefore Thomas' lord claimed the prisoner and rewarded him with 1,000 marks (£666) and a pension of 40 marks (£26 13s 4d) a year - a fraction of the prisoner's true worth.

By the time the king and his army had arrived at Caen they had already accumulated much booty, mainly from the rich drapery town of St. Lô, where 'no man could credit or imagine the great riches that were seized and plundered'. From Caen the ships were loaded with cloth, jewels, vessels of gold and silver and many other things which were shipped to England with the prisoners. These included 60 knights and over 300 wealthy citizens all worthy of ransom. The army remained at Caen for three days and then continued by way of Troarn, Rumesnil and Lisieux which they reached by 2 August; then on to Le Theil, Le Neubourg, Elboeuf and Pont-de-l'Arche on the River Seine. Towns on the route surrendered to the English host without pressure having heard of the sacking of Caen. By the time the army had reached the Seine the 300 Cheshire archers that had been requested had not arrived so an urgent summons was sent requesting a corps of the best one hundred to attend at once under the leadership of Sir William Brereton and to be at Sandwich by 13 August, ready to join the Prince, who was clearly not happy at their delay.

Edward's actions succeeded in drawing the large French army away from Aquitaine leaving the Earl of Derby master of south-west France. King Philip VI of France, alarmed at the situation, summoned his nobles and his army to St. Dennis and there the '*Oriflamme*', the French banner of war, was unfurled. With his army he then marched along the Seine to Rouen, the capital of Normandy, with the intention of cutting off the English army. On their march the French destroyed the bridges across the Seine in an effort to slow the English army's progress.

Edward arrived at the River Seine on 6 August, to find the bridges at Elbeuf and Pont-de-l'Arche destroyed. Attempting to find a suitable crossing he marched further inland towards Paris fully intending to cross to meet the Flemish troops and Hastings who were laying siege to Bethune. Meanwhile the French pursued the English on the other side of the river. The bridges at Léry, Gaillon, Vernon, Freneuse, and Épône were all down, but at Poissy, although partly destroyed, the piles and cross beams remained and so that the bridge could be repaired. Having arrived at Poissy on or about 11 August, Edward set his carpenters to work whilst the men-at-arms occupied themselves raiding the surrounding area. The carpenters repairing the bridge were often threatened by the French from the far bank but the Earl of Northampton and a party of men managed to cross on a make-shift bridge to defend them. A French chronicler told of the English atrocities: of them marching to Saint Germain-en-Láye on the outskirts of Paris, looting the town and burning the royal palace. They burned the villages of Nanterre, La Chaussée, Rueil and the tower of Mountjoie before marching to the walls of Paris. One of the raiding parties was led by the Prince of Wales and therefore one may assume that many of the Cheshire men were 'in on the action'.

On 16 August, the English army crossed the Seine and advanced north towards the River Somme. In five days the army advanced 70 miles along the road to Amiens, skirting the town of Beauvais, though burning its suburbs, and taking several small towns. Philip in close pursuit made better time and covered a similar distance in only three days. As before the French destroyed bridges in an effort to hem the invaders in. At Airaines the English army camped whilst scouts ventured out to find suitable places to cross the Somme. For three days they searched in vain. Edward decided to try to cross nearer the estuary, but to confuse the enemy he marched away from the river until he got to Oisemont where he again camped and again sent reconnaissance parties to find a crossing. A prisoner provided

Edward with the information he needed: at a place called Blanchetaque there was a ford at which, when the tide ebbed twice a day, men could wade across and where the river bottom was formed of white gravel which would make it easy for the heavy waggons to cross. However, the ford was below the town of Abbeville which was defended by an army of several thousand French under Sir Godemar du Fay.

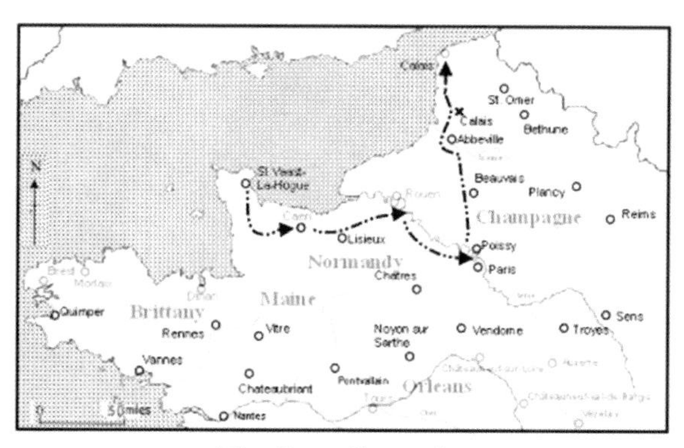

The Crecy Campaign

With the French host closing behind him, at mid-morning on Thursday, 24 August, Edward ordered his small army to cross. Archers, with their bows held high above their heads, were sent into the water whilst it was still waist high. They waded to within bow-shot of the northern bank where du Fay's men were drawn up to defend the crossing. Once across Hugh Despenser ordered his archers to stand in rows and to fire at a slight elevation, over the heads of the foremost ranks, at the enemy. Whilst the archers did their work, the English vanguard started to cross. The two Marshals of England followed their banners across the mile and a half of causeway, lances lowered ready for the fray. Northampton and Warwick then led their men into a desperate fight, many jousts occurred in the water, as many of the French knights eager for action had ridden into the river to meet the English. From the northern bank Genoese arbalesters (cross-bowmen) fired at the enemy, but the English archers out-shot them: their steady stream of arrows helped put the French to flight. The pursuit continued over a three-mile radius from the crossing point to Rue, Abbeville and Montreuil, many French being killed or captured.

Although Edward's army suffered heavy casualties they managed to cross before the tide changed and before King Philip's arrival.

Despite their heavy losses, the morale in the English army was high: from their earlier precarious position they were now relatively safe. To the religious the crossing must have seemed like another crossing of the Red Sea and if God was on their side and if a battle had to be fought now was the time. In fact battle was now inevitable so a good defensive position had to be found. Edward marched his army north-east to Crécy-en-Ponthieu and at the edge of woodland he found the position he needed. On a slope facing south into a shallow valley he arranged his army, which numbered about 14,000, and waited for the French. To the right of his position was a small river running through marshy ground, to the left the hamlet of Wadicourt and to his rear a small wood at the crest of the slope.

Edward divided his army into three battles, or divisions; the vanguard he placed near to the bottom of the slope, to its left and further up the slope he placed the second battle, leaving the rear-guard to command the top of the slope. The command of the vanguard was given to the young Prince - this was to be his first pitched battle. For his support the Prince was given the services of ten bannerets, including the experienced Earls of Warwick and Oxford, Godfrey de Harcourt, Sir Thomas Holland, Sir John Chandos, Sir James d'Audley of Stretton, Sir John de Folville, Sir Roger de Cheyney and Sir Bartholemew de Burghersh. Of the bannerets some had Cheshire connections: Chandos held estates in Cheshire; Audley of Stretton in Staffordshire was cousin to Audley of Helegh: Folville of Lincolnshire headed a family which settled about this time at Middlewich; Cheyney may have been related to Sir Alan Cheyney of Nantwich; and Burghersh, a Cornishman, was the Justiciar of Chester. In addition the Prince was served by 114 bachelors among whom were Sir Alexander de Venables, Sir Richard de Baskervylle and Sir Henry Praers, all from Cheshire. Also, the young Prince had the services of a number of nobles including Sir Richard de Stafford, a younger brother of Ralph, Earl of Stafford, leader of many Cheshire contingents. The Prince's total battle strength was 800 men-at-arms, 2,00 archers, and 1,000 spearmen.

The left flank, the second division, was commanded by the Earls of Northampton and Arundel and comprised of 500 men-at-arms and 1,200 archers. Of the men-at-arms, eleven were bannerets including Sir John le Strange of Whitchurch an extensive landowner in Cheshire and Sir James d'Audley of Helegh. Of the sixty-eight bachelors, six were out of the 'Cheshire stable': Sir John Trussel of Warmingham, Sir Richard Venables of Bollin, Sir John Haukestone of Wryneford, Sir Hamon Mascy of Potington, Sir John Delves of Doddington and Sir John Davenport of Davenport.

The King took the rear-guard of 700 men-at-arms and 2,000 archers, including thirty-one bannerets and 273 bachelors. Amongst the bachelors we find Sir Thomas Haukestone of Somerford, Sir Warine de Trussel of Warmingham, Sir Peter de Wetenhall, Sir Malcolm de Wasteneys of Taxall, and Sir Richard de Stanley. After positioning his army the King, dressed in green velvet and not his armour, rode among his army to encourage the men. At mid-day he issued orders for his men '*to eat heartily and to drink a glass; having done so they sat down on the grass with their helmets and weapons beside them, that they might be fresher when their enemies should arrive*'.

Unlike the English, the French army was in disarray with their troops lodged in various places and some still to arrive. Philip's intelligence was so poor that they almost marched past the English army and had to make a sudden change of course causing some confusion. It being late afternoon the French king decided to wait until the morning before giving battle: his methods of communication were also poor and part of his army prepared to do battle there and then.

At five o'clock on 26 August the French army began to charge. The Genoese arbalasters began to shoot but their bolts fell short. The English archers, positioned in their usual wedge formations, began to fire and so concentrated was their fire that 'it seemed as if it snowed. Their fire was accurate too and it put the French cross-bowmen to flight. The crossbow was a cumbersome weapon which took time to load and fire and was no match for the rapid firing longbow. Being positioned on a slope the English archer could fire horizontally and gain a good range and those in the rear ranks could easily fire over the heads of the others, thus producing a deadly effective cross-fire. On seeing the Genoese flee the French cavalry, thinking them deserters, rode them down, trampling them under the horses as they continued to charge towards the English lines and the Prince's division. The archers continued their fire. This time they aimed at the horses as once down they provided a serious obstacle to the following horses and the continuing cavalry charge. Now and again a unit of French cavalry would get through the hail of arrows and serious hand-to-hand fighting took place. The English man-at-arms fought on foot against the mounted enemy. The Welsh spearmen and those archers who had exhausted their supply of arrows, being un-encumbered by armour, nimbly ran between and under the horses slaying them to bring their riders down: alternatively, they speared the rider in his backside as he stood in his stirrups to fight - the seat of a man in armour being the least protected area.

A group of French knights succeeded in reaching the presence of the young Prince, who on two occasions fell to his knees. His standard bearer, Richard fitz Simon, had to rescue him by lashing around with his sword, keeping the banner under one foot and straddling the Prince shouting 'Edward and St. George, to the son of the King'. On one occasion whilst the standard bearer was thus engaged Sir Thomas Daniers of Bradley picked up the standard and held it aloft so that others would know where the Prince was. For his valour at Crécy in 'replanting the Prince's banner' as well as taking the Count of Tankerville at Caen, Sir Thomas was awarded an annuity of forty marks to be paid out of the issues of the Prince's manor of Frodsham, until a more convenient grant of land could be found for him. It was not until 1389 that lands were actually bestowed on the family in honour of the feat by which time Thomas was dead: the lands provided were at Hanley, near Macclesfield. In the sixteenth century the heralds allowed the family a special shield displaying an arm in armour holding a silver pennon against a black background strewn with silver stars to celebrate Sir Thomas' courage.

At one time in the battle the Prince's division was so hard pressed that assistance was sought from the King. Edward from his vantage point near the top of the hill could see that the battle was near to a close and refused help saying 'Let him take pains to win his spurs and to be worthy of the honour of knighthood which I so lately have conferred upon him. For I am resolved by the Grace of God that day shall be his and the honour shall rest with him'.

It was after dark before the French ceased to attack the English lines. In all they had made over a dozen separate attacks on the small English army. Since the Englishmen had been given their positions they had stood their ground and thus a small disciplined body of around 10,000 combatants defeated an army of at least 40,000. Strategy, a rare thing in the military events of the time, proved itself against military might. The skill of the common soldier, the archer, had proved itself against the proud aristocrats of France. On the morning after, when the clerks went out to count the cost of the battle, they found the valley was strewn with the dead: the valley between Wadicourt and Crécy is to this day known as the Vallée des Clercs. The French losses were heavy and the Chivalry of France had been sorely beaten, but the English losses were very slight in comparison, though the exact number of losses is not known for certain.

* * *

The names of some of the Cheshire men present at the famous Battle have already been mentioned, but what of the others, for 'in the vanguard there were many knights and squires of the county of Cestre in the Prince's company, and noble archers also'. We know that John Hyde, later Sir John, was there along with the two Crue brothers, as the following petition relates:

> *Petition from Thomas de Crue of the county of Cestre reminding the prince how he came to him [the Prince] at the Isle of Wyght in the cog Thomas, as he was crossing to Hoggis, and so to the battle of Cressy, and how the prince commanded through his serJohn IIts at arms, Raulyn Denys and William, that he and his brother should come on board his ship to serve with Sir John de Hyde. He received no wages for his labour at the battle of Cressy and when his brother was wounded at that battle and he went with him to succour him he received no reward. He is the prince's liegeman of the county of Cestre...*

The document dated in 1357 goes on to request a pardon for an offence of trespass. The names of the ordinary men-at-arms and archers are hard to trace but each family from each hundred of the County would have had a representative there.
Following its great victory the English army moved on towards Calais to regain communications with England and to lay siege to the important sea town which would give a footing for further activities. Although the French had received a sound thrashing further encroachments on their territory would have been a foolish enterprise for Edward's army was by this time weary and their numbers too small.

On Monday, 29 August, King Edward decamped and headed for Montreuil. The towns of Saint Josse, Neufchatel, Étaples and Rue were burnt and sacked. The following night the whole army camped at Wissant where they rested for a whole day before moving on to Calais. By the middle of September Calais was under siege by both the English army and its fleet. Edward settled down to starve the place into surrender. A large force of men were employed, around 30,000, and half of the country's shipping was employed in ferrying troops and supplies. To the west of the besieged town a 'village' was constructed to house the troops and some of their families. Here Edward held court and was joined by his wife, Queen Phillipa. On 12 September instructions were sent to Sir Thomas Ferrers, Justice of Chester, and to his lieutenant there requiring further men from Flint and Wales:

> *With the help of God the prince hath prospered in his present expedition and is now before Calays to besiege it. He now needs more Welsh to help him in the siege and the expedition he proposes to make aftyer it and therefore orders Sir Thomas to cause two hundred Welshmen to be chosen tried and arrayed in the countie of Flynt as well within the liberties of the bishop of St. Asaph as elsewhere, and to have them armed half with lances and other suitable arms, and half with bows and arrows so that they be at Dovre on Saturday the morrow of Michaelmas next. Griffith ap Jor' ap Meyler is to be their leader. This order is to be carried out without sparing anyone for gift or favour: and Sir Thomas is not to be so negligent or tardy in this matter as he was in the last array of archers of Cestre.*

A similar request was sent to the Justice of South Wales. It appears that the prince was still not happy about the array of the three hundred Cheshire archers ordered in July and again in August. On 14 September orders were issued to the Chamberlain of Chester, requiring him to purchase cloth for the archers of Flint, it continues: *"He is to pay Sir William Brereton, leader of the one hundred archers which the prince has ordered to come to him, his wages for the seven days spent in coming with the said archers, to wit two shillings a day".*

It would appear that Brereton's elite corps finally met the English army at Calais in early September. The siege went on and on through the winter and into the spring of 1347, when efforts were made to raise more troops to relieve the weary besiegers. On 6 March the Prince issued orders to Sir Thomas Danyers to cause him to come to him.

> *... with all haste to Caleys according to his retainder and to chose and bring with him at the prince's cost one hundred of the best archers he can find so that he be with the prince on Palm Sunday next at the latest. The Chamberlain of Cestre has been ordered to clothe the said archers and to pay him and*

them their wages for fourteen days until their arrival with the prince...

Similar orders were issued to Alexander de Wasteneys 'of the county of Cestre', William de Tabley, Ralphe de Oldyngton and Ralph de Stathum. On the same date the sheriff of Flint, Richard del Hough was ordered to array one hundred Welshmen, and the Justice of North Wales one hundred, half of whom were to be archers and the others armed with a lance. On 8 March 1,200 Welshmen were ordered from North Wales, half of them again were to be archers, and the others spearmen. On that same date a further one hundred were ordered from Cheshire. Sir Thomas Danyers took with him to Calais three squires and because no mention of them was made in the initial order, the Chamberlain refused to pay them. Danyers appealed to the Prince, and on 21 March, John de Burnham was ordered to pay them:

...as he has refused to pay the wages of the esquires of Sir Thomas Danyers, because no mention of such wages was made in the prince's letter ordering him to pay sir Thomas Danyers two shillings a day for his wages for fourteen days in coming to the prince – to pay Sir Thomas fourteen days wages for the two esquires of his retinue, as well as for the third esquire who is to be captain of the one hundred archers who are to be brought to the prince by Sir Thomas, to wit for each of them twelve pence a day. He is to pay Sir Thomas Danyers ten pounds for arrears of his fee."

On 9 March an enquiry was held into the amount of land held by Sir William de Brereton, who had died some time earlier so perhaps he died during the siege of Calais. The deed relates to the fact that he held the manor of Brereton by knight's service to Hugh Venables, baron of Kinderton and that his heir was his son, another William.

John Hyde of Hyde returned home after the Battle of Crécy but on 12 September 1346 he received letters of protection (letters which protected a man from legal process whilst abroad in the King's service). He received his letters on going abroad with, or in the service of, the Prince of Wales. In the document, John is styled Sir John so, as this is the first occasion of him being so styled, it may be that he was knighted at the Battle of Crécy; it was common practice to dub new knights immediately before or just after a major battle. On 14 March 1347, an indenture was issued retaining 'Sir John de la

Hyde' to the service of the Prince for one year; he was required to serve with two esquires, at a fee of £20, with compensation for any war horses he might lose. The mediaeval war horse, 'destrier', was a valuable item costing as much as £100 and many such horses were bred on the Prince's estates at Macclesfield.

In view of the fact that Queen Isabella journeyed to Calais it may be assumed that Robert Fouleshurst of Crewe a 'yeoman of the princes lady mother, the queen', was there with the steward of her household, Thomas Haukeston of Smallwood. During May 1347 Sir Richard Baskervylle. was ordered to be at Dover or Sandwich by the octave of Trinity with men-at-arms for service at Calais.

In July of the same year a French relieving army arrived at Calais, but on seeing the size of the English host, they turned away. On seeing their countrymen leave the Governors of Calais realised their hopes of rescue had gone and therefore gave the town up. Edward had, in capturing Calais, created a useful footing in France for future expeditions. From here the Prince of Wales and his troops, many of whom were either Cheshire men or Welsh men, set off on raids to control the immediate neighbourhood until on 2 September a truce was declared to give both sides breathing space.

The truce of 1341 was to have expired in the Spring of 1348 but by common agreement it was extended until 1350 due to the outbreak of the Black Death. Disease was rife throughout Europe and both England and France lost a third of their populations: military activity was the last thing either side wanted.

* * *

References for Chapter One

The Black Prince's Register, parts I, 1346-8, and III, 1351-65, published by the Deputy Keeper of the Public Records, has been used for examples of recruitment, payments, rewards, clothing, letters of protection, and offices of Cheshire people. Various versions of *The Chronicles of John Froissart* are used for examples of the campaigns from his contemporary accounts. Details of those serving at Crécy have been obtained from *Rymer's Foedera*, and G. Wrottesley, *Crécy and Calais* (1898). The following are general works of reference used for the first edition: G. Ormerod, *History of the County Palatine of Cheshire*, ed. Helsby (1898); A. Bryant, *The Age of Chivalry* (1963); H.J.Hewitt, *Cheshire Under the Three Edwards* (1967); H. Cole, *The Black Prince* (1976); B. Emerson, *The Black Prince* (1976); A.H. Burne, *The Crécy*

War (1955); M. McKisack, *The Fourteenth Century*, (1959). J. Sumption, *Trial by Battle: The Hundred Years War, Vol. 1* (1999) - the first of an excellent series on the Hundred Years Wars which has been consulted for this second edition.

*   *   *

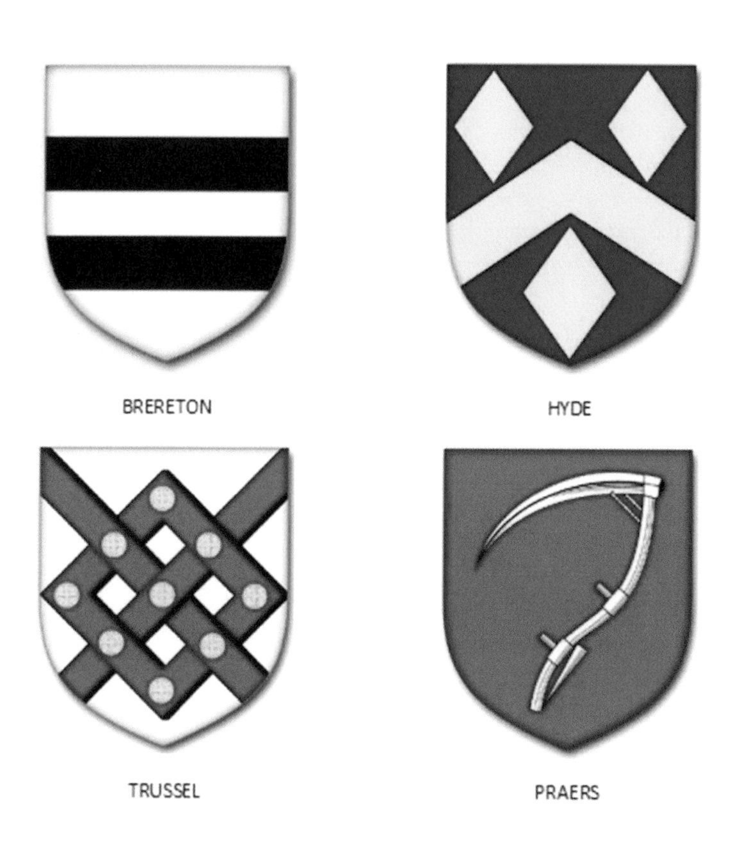

2. CALVELEY AND KNOLLES

Hostilities started again in the Spring of 1350 when the French attempted to re-take Calais. The deputy governor of the port was bribed by the French to open the gates to a French raiding party. The plot was betrayed and Edward, Prince of Wales, with a hand-picked body of men surprised the French raiding party and captured all of them.

In August, the same year a small fleet of ships manned by archers and men-at-arms were assembled, at Sandwich, to pursue and capture a Castilian fleet of pirates who had been raiding English merchant vessels. On 29 August, the enemy were sighted off Dungeness: the sea battle that followed was a victory for the English archers who out-shot the Spanish crossbowmen making the task of the boarding parties easier.

The war with France was to be renewed in earnest for their new king, John II, intended to be rid of the English once and for all. The war during the first half of the decade was spasmodic, there being no real campaigns or battles. In the years between 1350 and 1355, some Cheshire men were active in France: Sir John Griffith (or Griffin) of Barterton received letters of protection on 4 May 1352 on going to Gascony with Sir Ralph de Stafford, Earl of Stafford; Sir John Hyde was active throughout 1351 and 1352 with a command of seventy-one archers; Robert de Legh of Adlington served in France throughout the period; and finally, there were the two most celebrated Cheshire knights Hugh de Calveley and Robert Knolles.

Both Hugh and Robert began their military careers some ten years earlier and became heroes of the age of chivalry and legends throughout Europe in their own times. Not only were they Cheshire men but they were probably related – cousins or even half-brothers. Both amassed great fortunes and if anything, Sir Robert became the greater of the two. Their careers and adventures will feature in most of the chapters which follow.

Hugh Calveley was born around 1325, the eldest son of Richard de Calveley who held the manor of Calveley. Between 1341 and 1364 he was active in the civil war in Brittany and served under the banner of Sir Thomas Dagworth taking part in the *chevauchées* across Brittany in the winter and Spring of 1345-46, seeing service at the siege of La Roche-Derrien on 1 December 1345, and also at the battle of St. Pol-de-Léon. Whether he fought at the battle of Crécy is not known for sure. As a result of successes in Brittany, Dagworth was promoted to the position of knight banneret and fifty of his men were made bachelors and these may have included Hugh Calveley. On 12 July 1347, he was at the siege of Durianum, again under Dagworth's command, with a total force of eighty men-at-arms and 400 archers.

Hugh Calveley is next heard of as one of the participants in the 'Battle of the Thirty' fought on 27 March 1351. At the time he was garrisoned at Pleoërmel in Brittany with Sir Richard Brembro (or Bremborough) the captain of the castle. Shortly after Dagworth had been slain in an ambush and incensed by the tragic loss of their leader, the garrison at Ploërmel pillaged the surrounding area. In the neighbouring castle of Josselin, a Franco-Breton force under Sir Robert de Beaumanoir was garrisoned who on hearing of the English atrocities sallied out to attack Ploërmel. However, Sir Robert and Sir Richard agreed to confer with one another and discuss their respective points of view: Sir Robert talking of the great wrongs committed by the Anglo-Breton forces and Sir Richard arguing that his cause was just as the Franco-Breton forces were responsible for the killing of old Dagworth. To settle matters it was decided to hold a joust of two or three of the best knights from each side. Brembro suggested a trial by combat of thirty men-at-arms from each side and this was accepted. Accordingly sixty warriors from the two forces made their way to a level piece of ground between the two castles.' The battle was fought at a place called Mi-Voie. The English side consisted of twenty-two Bretons and eight Englishmen: Sir Richard Brembro, Sir Hugh Calveley, Sir Robert Knolles, Sir Richard de la Lande, Sir Thomas Belifort, Sir Thomas Haulton, John Trussel and John Plessington. Of the eight men three were certainly from Cheshire, Sir Hugh, Sir Robert, and John Trussell. It might be that Haulton was from Halton, Cheshire, and that 'Brembro' is a corruption of the Cheshire place-name Bromborough. It is also similar to that of Thomas Brembre a Cheshire man who had letters of protection issued on 1 May 1341.

The encounter was fierce and exhausting and after four Frenchmen and two English lay dead a rest period was taken; the combatants resting under a large oak tree which stood in the middle of the field. At the end of the second half the Anglo-Breton force were defeated. Sir Richard, the commander lay dead, and others including Calveley and Knolles were taken to Josselin as prisoners to await ransom. Both Calveley and Knolles were soon released, and continued their activities in Brittany's guerilla war.

* * *

Late in 1353 Hugh returned to Cheshire for in January 1354, he together with a number of other local men were pardoned for all felonies, trespasses and 'outlawries' committed prior to l0 September 1353. On 8 July 1354 Sir Hugh was granted letters of protection on returning to Brittany on the King's service. The following Cheshire men were also granted protection from civil litigation, as about to join Sir Hugh's company: William de Crue, Nicholas de Vernon, William de Bulkylegh de Alpraham the younger, John son of Robert de Seint Pierre, Peter son of John de Wetenhale de Minshull, John ie Bruyn, John Gandy, Edmund de Coghull and Hugh, son of David de Crue.

In the Autumn, Hugh and his men were at Bécherel, Brittany, when he heard of a fête to be held at the Castle of Montmuran in honour of a Breton knight Sir Bertram du Guesclin, an aggressive and skilful warrior. Guesclin's record of atrocities made him much feared in the English camps and was to the English what Calveley and Knolles were to become to the French. Sir Hugh decided to intercept the Breton warrior on his route to the castle but unfortunately Guesclin somehow heard of the planned ambush and managed to 'turn the tables' and capture Hugh. Robert Knolles was born around the same time as Sir Hugh though his date of birth has been put as early as 1317, which seems unlikely. His family background is somewhat obscure. An inquiry into the lands held by Mabel de Calveley, mother of Hugh, mentions Robert de 'Knollus' and styles him as a *chevalier* - knight. The document dated 1363 reads:

> *...Mabel de Calvylegh held for life the manor of Lee, with appurtences by the demise of John de Wingfeld, chevalier, from the Earl of Chester in capite by military service, with reversion to Hugh de Calveley, knight, and his heirs of his body, with remainder to David de Calvlylegh, his brother in tail, remainder to Robert de Knollus, chr., in tail, with final remainder to the right heirs of the said Sir Hugh de Calvlylegh for ever. Val. p. annum xl."*

When the estate of Lee was granted to Mabel by Sir John de Wingfield in May 1354, with authority from the Earl of Chester, it was with remainders to 'Hugh, David, and Robert, sons of Richard de Calvylegh, with an ultimate remainder to the right heirs of the said Hugh'. clearly Hugh was the eldest son and David and Robert younger sons. Is this Robert the same as Robert Knolles? It may be given the information in a third document dated 10 April 1354 which was addressed to the Chamberlain of Chester:

> *...Order to the same to cause charters to be made out in due form, quit of the fee of seal in execution of a grant by the prince to his bachelor Sir John de Wengefeld of a licence to give and grant the manor of Lee, county Chester, held of the prince in chief, to Mabel de Calvylegh and Henry de Neuton, chaplain, for life with successive remainders in tail to Hugh de Calvylegh, the elder, David de Calvylegh, the elder, and Robert son of Richard de Knolles; and the remainder to the right heirs of Hugh...*

On Knolles relationship to Calveley, Lysons in his *Magna Brittania* declares:

> *It is a singular circumstance that Sir Hugh Calveley, should have had a nephew named Robert Knolles, the son of his sister Eve, who married Richard. Knolles, on which Robert, the manor of Lea, in case of failure of issue male from Sir Hugh Calveley and his brother David was entailed........."*

Whatever the case, they seem to have been closely related but their characters were dissimilar. Hugh was a giant of a man with projecting cheek bones, a receding hair line, red hair and long teeth. He had a large appetite, eating as much as four men and drinking as much as ten. He was kind and chivalrous, honoured among men and of great strength. Perhaps a religious man, for whenever he seized booty he had it sprinkled with Holy Water to absolve him of his sins in taking it! He later became a generous benefactor to the church.

Robert Knolles was small in stature, but a tough and skilled warrior and, though of few words, a skilful diplomat. Like Hugh, in later life made many charitable donations to the Church. The arms of the two men do not show any family connections; *Calveley bore: Argent, a fess Gules, between three calves, tripant, Sable*. (A silver shield with a thick red bar between three black calves). Knolles bore: *Gules, on a chevron, Argent, three roses of the field*. (A red shield, with a silver chevron, with three red roses thereon). Their crests were, respectively, a black calf's head set in a duke's coronet, and, a silver ram's head with gold horns. The arms borne by Knolles once appeared on Sir Hugh's tomb at Bunbury and Sir Hugh's arms appear in the church at Sculthorpe, Norfolk, which endowed by Sir Robert. His military career followed that of Sir Hugh's very closely. Both were at La Roche Derrien, at St. Pol de Léon and at the Battle of the Thirty. The two men seem to have parted company shortly after the Battle of the Thirty. Following the death of Dagworth, Sir William Bentley succeeded as the King's Lieuteuant, or Viceroy, in Brittany and Robert served under his command. Early in 1352 Robert took a part in the capture of Fougères from the Breton knight Bertram du Guesclin and consequently was installed as its captain by Bentley. Following the capture of the castle Bentley returned home leaving Robert there. With Bentley's departure the French laid siege to Fougères in an effort to retake it and Knolles found himself in a desperate situation with only a handful of men to garrison the place. Bentley hearing the news hurried back to Brittany to rescue his comrade and was successful in putting the French to flight and destroying the siege towers which had been erected around the castle walls.

* * *

Throughout the summer Sir William Bentley set about strengthening the Duchy's defences: meanwhile King John II was gathering an army intent upon throwing the English out of Brittany. The French armies were commanded by Guy de Nesle, a Marshal of France, who was given the title of Governor General of Brittany. In August 1352 Nesle invaded the duchy with an initial objective of taking the port of Brest in the far west. He took Rennes, having by-passed Fougères on route. Bentley then marshalled his forces at Ploërmel and on hearing of the fall of Rennes he and his deputy, Robert Knolles, marched to intercept the French on their way to Brest. On 14 August the Anglo-Breton army marched to meet the French, who numbered about 3,000. At noon that day Sir William and Sir Robert entered the town of Mauron from where they sighted to the north-east the French advance and sought a suitable site to give battle.

A suitable ground was found on a spur projecting from a ridge on which the town of Mauron was situated. The spur sloped gently down to the river level in the east and then sloped up gently again towards the village of St. Léry. On the crest of the spur there was a line of trees, to its right a small fortified house and to the left a steeper slope down to the Rennes road. Bentley dismounted his troops in front of the line of trees and around the edge of the spur. They formed up in usual fashion of men-at-arms flanked by archers over a frontage of seven hundred yards: they numbered slightly less than the French. Nesle on seeing the English formed up and waiting for him took the unusual step of having his force dismount, except for a division under the Count of Hangest. Feeling confident in having the superior force, the French commander sent heralds with terms for an English surrender, but Bentley rejected them.

At four o'clock in the afternoon the battle began with the French cavalry charging the English right and putting the archers on that flank to flight. Having lost their cover, the men-at-arms on the right flank backed up to the line of trees to make a defensive stand. Because of the steep slopes the archers on the left flank were not harassed by cavalry and used their bows to good effect and put the French right wing to flight. After they had loosed all their arrows the archers charged, swords in hand, after the French men-at-arms. Suddenly the archers veered to their right and fell on the French centre, causing havoc. The men-at-arms who were fighting off the French cavalry in the trees, saw the events in mid-field and with renewed vigour fought on and eventually forced the cavalry back, step by step, down the slope. During the battle Bentley was fatally wounded, and Knolles took command and brought the battle to a successful conclusion. Guy de Nesle was slain and several hundred of his knights were either slain or taken prisoner. These included 45 of France's new order of Chivalry, the Order of the Star, an order of which Nesle was a co-founder with King John II, in imitation of King Edward's Order of the Garter.

Once again, a small disciplined force had overcome a much superior yet dis-organised one. The French had been split and consequently fell prey to the English archer who made up two-thirds of the Anglo-Breton army. After the battle, which lasted no more than a few hours, Knolles had the archers who fled at the start rounded up and had thirty of them executed for desertion. The Battle of Mauron left the English masters of Brittany, therefore for a few years there were no other engagements of note. Knolles' reputation as a soldier was gained by this victory and from this time on he earned great renown.

From 1353 both Calveley and Knolles continued to harass the French in Brittany and Normandy. The two became experts in the art of war and became so successful that many Englishmen and Bretons were drawn to their service. They took many prisoners worthy of ransom and much valuable booty becoming very wealthy men. The numbers they attracted to their companies became much greater due to their qualities of largesse. Sir Robert became the captain of many castles in Brittany and Normandy including Fougères and Châteaubriant.

* * *

References for Chapter Two

The Black Prince's Register, parts I and III, have references as to the relationship of the two men, and various letters of protection. *The Chronicles of John Froissart*, for some of the exploits. *Rymer's Foedera* for the castles occupied by Knolles. Otterbourne states that both were at St. Pol de Léon and La Roche Derrien. *The History of Cheshire*, vol. II by Ormerod gives details of Calveley's family. *The Crécy War* by Burne covers the period admirably. J. Sumption, *Trial by Battle: The Hundred Years War, Volume 1* (1999) and *Trial by Fire: The Hundred Years War, Volume 2* (2001) - the first and second of the excellent series on the Hundred Years Wars have been consulted for this second edition. My book *Dogs of War* details the careers of both Hugh Calveley and Robert Knolles.

* * *

DANIERS

GRIFFIN

CALVELEY

KNOLLES

3. CHEVEAUCHÉES

The hostilities with France continued in 1355 and in that year England's activity amounted to a fast ride with the intention of wasting southern France. The following year another *chevauchée* was made into western France which culminated in the famous battle of Poitiers. The activities of the Cheshire people in the two years are well recorded, from knight to archer and common soldier.

The peace arranged in 1347 had been continually broken and was renewed in 1350 and 1352. Both countries realised that a major conflict was inevitable and in 1354 negotiations were held in an effort to continue the truce. King Edward stated that he would drop his claim to the French throne in exchange for the complete sovereignty of the provinces of Guienne, Ponthieu, Brittany and Normandy; or in place of the latter, Flanders. The French on hearing of the English proposals rejected them completely.

King Edward decided to invade France once again and bring them to heel. He planned a campaign on three fronts; from the south-west, the north, and north-east. Of the three fronts, only one actually succeeded. The north-eastern campaign had to be abandoned as the King, who led it, had to return to deal with a Scots invasion of northern England. The northern campaign, which was to have been led by the Duke of Lancaster, never started because of lack of support from Charles, King of Navarre, a substantial landowner in Normandy. As a young man of twenty-five Prince Edward of Wales was given absolute command of the south-western attack and by spring of 1355 he had started to make his plans. In May orders were issued to the administrators of the county of Chester to array skilful archers. The senior administrator of the county at this time was Sir Bartholemew de Burghersh, as Justiciar; his lieutenant was John de Delves, of Doddington. An order issued on 21 May was sent to Delves and the Chamberlain of Chester, John de Burnham, was in respect of certain previous correspondence between them and the Prince's adviser, Sir John de Wingfield (Wengefeld):

> *...to test and array two hundred of the best and most skilful archers from all the hundreds of the said county in whosoever lordship they be for the prince wills that he be served before all others. Then they are to choose the hundred best and most skilful archers of the said county, touching whom Sir John Danyers,*

Sir Ralph de Modberley, and the other esquires who have been with the prince in London, have been ordered by the prince to give them information...

The order is clearly asking for a select band of one hundred archers, and shows that prior to their recruitment local leaders had been in London to advise the Prince. The command continues:

... In as much as there are few archers in the forest of Wirhale, the prince wills that Hamonet Mascy an Goldesburgh 'le frere' be leaders of the archers of the hundred of Broxon ...

Throughout the county there went a general proclamation that every man between the ages of sixteen and sixty should assemble and be tested for service with the Prince, their Earl and that:

...no one on pain of forfeiture of whatever he could forfeit, should engage himself' to go to war in any company except the prince's without the prince's special leave, until the prince should be assured of as many archers as he needs...

The next document concerning recruitment, is dated the same day; it is issued by the prince, to Delves and Burnham and concerns the payments of the leaders of archers:

...in as much as an agreement has been reached between the prince and Sir Ralph de Modberley, Sir John Danyers, William de Carenton, Hamon Mascy, John Danyers, Thomas de Stathum, Robert le Bruyn, and Robert de Legh 'le fitz', as to their next year's fees for the war, and the prince wills that they be paid a moiety of their fees in hand...
Sir Ralph de Modberley £11 13s 4d.
Sir John Daniers £11 13 4d
William de Karenton 10 marks
Hamon Mascy 100 shillings
John Danyers 100 shillings
Thomas de Stathum 100 shillings
Robert le Bruyn 66s 8d
Robert, son of Robert de Legh 66s 8d
Order, also, to allow £11 13s 4d to Sir John Danyers, out of the debt which he is bound to pay the prince at Midsummer next, in full payment of his entire fee for next year....... Order also to cause letters of protection, with clause volumus, to be made out in favour of the above persons and others of those

parts who are to go in the prince's company, to last from the quinzane of Trinity next, for a year...

The following day the Chamberlain was ordered to go to London with what money he could, to help finance the coming expedition. He was, however, to make sure he left sufficient behind to pay those arrayed, and indeed to make sure enough cloth had been bought to clothe them. On 13 June Sir John Griffyn of Barterton, near Nantwich, was granted payment of twenty marks, as a moiety (half) of his fee if he was bringing two esquires with him, '*...and £11 3 s. 4d. to wit a moiety of his fee of £23 6s. 8d. if he is coming with one...*' The following day letters of protection were ordered for Thomas d'Ardern on going to Gascony with Sir Richard Stafford. On 25 June, Richard de Mascy and Hamon de Ashlee were granted half of their fees of ten marks per annum. Extra archers were ordered on 26 June:

...it amplification of previous orders to him (Burnham) and the lieutenant of the justice of Cestre to send three hundred archers of the county of Cestre to the prince at Plymouth. by three weeks from Midsummer, to send one hundred archers of the county of Flynt in addition to the above three hundred, paying all of them three weeks wages it hand at the rate of 6d a day for the archers of Cestre and 3d a day for the archers of Flynt, and delivering to them white and green cloth for their 'cotecourtepiz' and hats as formerly. The prince wills that the following persons be the leaders of the archers of the various hundreds:
Sir John de Hide and Robert son of Robert de Legh - Mackersfield, a moiety each;
Robert Bruyn - Edesbury;
Hamon de Mascy of Pudington and Hugh Golbourn - Wirhale & Broxen a moiety each;
Sir John Griffyn - Wych Malbank;
and that each knight of the above leaders have 2s a day for his wages from the time of leaving home until his arrival at Plymuth, and each esquire 1s a day for the same period. The wages to be paid out of the common fine of Cheshire and the subsidy of the county of Flynt...

During June 1355, the Prince heard that some of his subjects of Cheshire, Flint and North Wales, had joined the retinues of other nobles, '*in defiance of his general proclamation*'. He accordingly ordered his administrators to seize the lands and goods of the men and of those who had procured their service, and to keep them seized until further notice. Throughout June and July letters of protection and orders to suspend litigation were issued in favour of those about to leave for south-east France, for example, Robert de Fouleshurst on 28 June; William le Vernoun de Gostre on 4 July; Sir John Tochet, who went in the Earl of Warwick's retinue; Robert de Acton on 30 July; and to *the men of the county of Cestre who were to go with Henry of Lancaster*, on 1 July.

On 10 July, Prince Edward was appointed the King's Lieutenant for Gascony. As such he signed an indenture to maintain a personal retinue of 433 men-at-arms, 400 mounted archers and 300 foot archers. The greatest proportion of this retinue of just over eleven hundred were Cheshire men. In addition to the prince's company the Earls of Warwick, Suffolk, Oxford and Salisbury, with Sir John de Lisle and Sir Reginald de Cobham each had retinues, making a total force of around 3,000 men. During the month of August the army gathered on the south coast whilst adequate shipping was found. Further letters of protection were issued to Cheshire men who were about to join the prince: Alan Cheyenne of Nantwich, Simon de Grimsditch, John Starky, John de Merebury, John de Neuton, Geofrey de Stanlegh, William de Chorley and Richard Bowere de Knotesford - to name but a few. Although most men seem to have been prepared to go, others were not as some fell ill, deserted, or just failed to arrive. On l5 August 1355 an order was sent to Delves and the Chamberlain:

> *... inasmuch as Thomas de Brescy, who was chosen among other archers of the said county to go beyond the seas with the prince and has received cloth of the suit of his fellow archers, has not yet joined the prince, to charge him to come to the prince with all speed, and if he excuses himself on any ground, pretend or otherwise, or tries to avoid being found, to take his body as soon as possible and put him in safe keeping in the castle of Cestre until further order...*

Orders were issued to arrest Richard de Wynstanston and his colleagues, who had deserted with £6 cash on 26 August. Twenty-one men from Flint, fourteen from North Wales and four from Cheshire left the army having been paid and issued with uniform. An order dated 5 September was issued naming the four Cheshire men as William Dodefyn, Thomas de Brescy. John de Pulford, and

Richard de Wynstanston (again) and stating that they should be arrested. It would appear that de Brescy, having been found, and having joined the King, soon decided that the army life was not for him. Some men fell ill and after certification by their leaders were allowed home on the Prince's writ, for example, on 2 September, Roger de Bechyngton, Richard de Codyngton, Richard de Codecote, William Bakere, Utrich de Huxiegh, Ken Says; and on 7 September, John Boidell de Lyme, David de Overton, Randolph de Bagelegh. with four others from Flint and four from North Wales.

* * *

On 9 September, the expeditionary force under the command of the Prince of Wales in his capacity as Lieutenant of the Duchy of Aquitaine, set sail and after eleven days the English army disembarked at Bordeaux. Their mission was to seize into the King's hands all lands, towns, castles and franchises. Having arrived in Bordeaux the Prince summoned the Gascon nobility to swear fealty to the Crown of England. Of all the Gascons to attend the Prince at his headquarters in the Abbey de St. Andre, the most powerful was the Captal de Buch. Following the initial formalities the English and the Gascons set about planning their strategy.

On 5 October, an allied force of around 5,000 set off on their first *chevauchée* through the territories of Count John II d'Armagnac who had done so much to attempt to re-take the English possessions in the south of France. They had decided in fact to ride from coast to coast, right across southern France. From Bordeaux the army marched south following the River Garonne until they reached the frontier with the enemy territory. From the frontier, just south of Arouille, which they reached on the sixth day, the army marched in its battle formation. The vanguard was led by the Earl of Warwick, with Reginald de Cobham as Constable; the centre was led by the Prince, with the Earl of Oxford, Burghersh (the Justiciar of Chester) and the Capital de Buch ; the rearguard was led by the two Earls, Suffolk and Salisbury. The English host unfurled its banners and set about devastating the area. On reaching Plaissance, nearly one hundred miles out from base, the army moved east. They marched under the nose of the Count who was garrisoned at Toulouse and on to Carcassonne where they took part of the town and rested for a few days. On 2 November, they fired the town and departed, still heading east. Six days later the army were within ten miles of the

Mediterranean sea, when they heard that the French forces were gathering in their rear to cut them off.

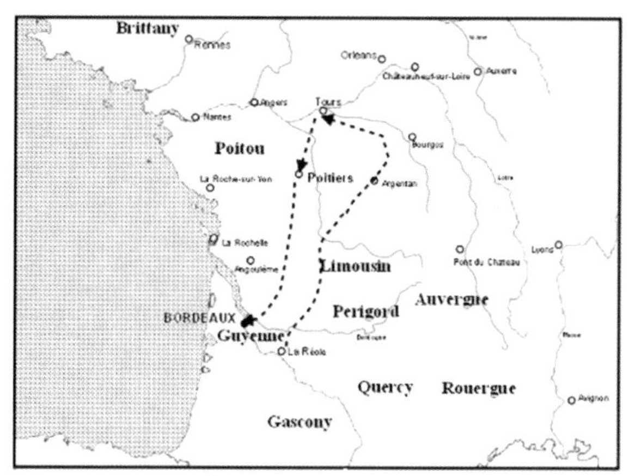

The Poitiers Campaign

On receiving intelligence as to the French activities, Edward decided to turn back, though initially he marched north for a few miles with the idea of deceiving the French as to his real intentions. The actual march home started on 10 November and followed a route further south than before until he was beyond Carbonne when he headed north. As the army got beyond Toulouse the French ventured out of their garrison, as if to chase the retreating English. Edward turned to face his enemy and sent Burgersh, Sir John Chandos, and Sir James Audley, to locate them. On meeting the enemy the small party charged them, took two hundred prisoners and sent the rest scurrying back to Toulouse. Following their success on Friday 20 November, the army continued its progress home reaching La Réole by 2 December.

The '*grande chevauchée*' as it is known was a triumph for the young Prince of Wales. Morale in the army had remained high throughout as there had been much plunder for the troops to seize. The Anglo-Gascon army had dealt the French a severe blow, without a major engagement: they had ridden through six hundred miles of enemy territory in nine weeks without hindrance. Most of the men of Cheshire and Flint settled down to spend Christmas at Bordeaux with the prince. Some of with the Earl of Warwick at La Role, whilst others may have been with Salisbury at Sainte-Foy-la-Crande, or Suffolk at Saint Emilion. No doubt some men returned home to

Cheshire as did William Jodrell whose leave pass, sealed by the Prince, still survives and reads:

> *Know all that we, the Prince of Wales, have given leave on the day of the date of this instrument to William Jauderel, one of our archers, to go to England. In witness of this we have caused our seal to be placed on this bill. Given at Bordeaux l6th of December in the year of grace 1355.*

Christmas was spent in 'great joy and solace...there was gaiety, noblesse, courtesy, goodness. and largesse'. Following the Christmas holiday the business of war had to be continued. In the middle of January, 1356, the Prince moved his headquarters twenty miles inland to Libourne. From this new base he sent raiding parties into French territory: Burghersh, as far as Congnac and Saintonge; Chandos and Audley to Agen; Warwick reached Tonneins and Clairac; and the Earls of Suffolk and Salisbury reached Rocamadour. The pressure on the French was intense, but the English met no resistance despite the count of Armagnac being garrisoned at Agen. Chandos and Audley with their men, some of whom were from Cheshire, were allowed to plunder and devastate the area. The Prince and the Captal de Buch rode as far as Périgueux where, despite an offer of cash, they sacked the town. The bribe was rejected in the following words, as related by the chronicler Froissart 'the King of England is rich..... and he desires only to do that which he has set out to do, which is to punish, discipline and tame all inhabitants of the Duchy of Aquitaine, who have rebelled against my father'.

Throughout the winter months of 1356 the Prince continued to punish the people of Aquitaine. Having induced the peoples of south-west France to his cause he began to plan his invasion into the heart of France. Men and supplies would be needed but, firstly, the troops he already had required payment. A pay roll dated 2 January, written at Bordeaux names some Cheshire men, for example: Hamo Mascy, leader of 63 archers was paid £11 8s 6d; John Daniers was paid £4 1s for himself and eighteen archers who were to stay in Bordeaux whilst the others went on raids; Ralph Mobberley was paid £7 4s for his charge of 32 archers; Robert Bruyn with 28 archers received £6 6s; John Hide had £B 6s 6d for 37 archers. On 29 February 1356. the administrators of Cheshire were informed that the Earl of Chester

> *...on account of his urgent need of bows, arrows and bow strings in the parts of Gascony, has sent Robert Pipot of Broukford to England to buy and purvey for his use a thousand sheaves of*

arrows and four hundred gross of bow-strings, but no arrows can be obtained from England, because the King has caused to be arrested and taken for his use all the arrows that can be found anywhere there, so that the Prince is now sending the said Robert to the parts of Cestre... to arrest the fletchers themselves to continue working at their craft for the prince, until he is satisfied.

Men were summoned by the following order to Delves:

... in as much as the King has ordained that three hundred archers be sent speedily: to the prince in Gascony in the company of Sir Richard Destafford and wills that two hundred of them be from the county of Cestre, and the remainder from elsewhere as ordered, to cause two hundred of the best mounted archers they can find to be chosen, tested and arrayed with all possible speed in the said county to appoint two suitable persons of the said county to be their leaders, so that they may be at Plymuth with out fail on Palm Sunday (16 April) ready to cross with Sir Richard...

The last document is dated 15 March and goes on to say that the leaders be paid 12d a day and the archers 6d a day. In November 1355, 100 were ordered to muster at Newcastle under Lyme by Christmas Day ready to go to south-west France. On 26 March 1356, a further instruction was sent out for a further 300, a third of whom were to be found in Cheshire; these too had to be at Plymouth by Palm Sunday. In view of the numbers already in France, the recruitment of a further 300 Cheshire men in the spring of 1356 appears a hopeless task. Some of the men newly recruited would have been men who, like Jodrell, had returned to their homes for the winter months: some of the new recruits would have been barely sixteen years old. Of the 1356 recruits we have Robert de Acton, Thomas Donne de Crowton, David Seys de Egge and Thomas son of Thomas Wolfall all of whom were granted letters of protection on going to Gascony to serve the Prince. A few months earlier, Sir John Danyers and Thomas Elensone de Bulkylegh had letters of protection on going to Gascony.

* * *

Whilst Prince Edward was gathering his troops in the spring and summer, Henry, Duke of Lancaster was preparing to go to Brittany with its new Duke. On learning of news that the King of Navarre was having trouble with the King of France over his lands in Normandy, Lancaster prepared to go to his aid. In May he set sail for Normandy with the objective of relieving the cities of Evreux, Pont Audemer and Breteuil which were holding out against the French king. Henry gathered an army of 500 men-at-arms and 800 archers, many of whom may have been from Cheshire as the duke held estates in the county, for example, the Barony of Halton. Having arrived at La Hogue the Duke awaited support from the King of Navarre's brother with a small force of loyal Normans. At the beginning of June Sir Robert Knolles met Lancaster at Montebourg: he had with him 300 men-at-arms and 500 archers. Sir Robert had come from Brittany where he had been fully engaged for the past five years.

On 22 June Lancaster set off on his mission leaving some of Sir Robert's men behind to defend the Normandy peninsula. The mission was completed in fifteen days and encountered the French on only once, and then he decided discretion was the better part of valour and slipped away under the cover of darkness. On their return, Sir Robert and seven of his men-at-arms were not far from their base at Montebourg when about 120 Franch men-at-arms attacked them thinking them an easy target. The French were wrong: Knolles put them to flight after many of them had been killed and three taken prisoner - one of many valiant acts for which he became famous: it is no wonder that the French called him the 'terrible Robert'.

Having completed his Normandy operation Lancaster set off into the province of Maine intending to embark on his original mission and if possible, to meet the Prince of Wales who was marching north. The Prince's second *chevauchée* set off on 4 August 1356 with around 6,000 men, many of whom were Gascons. Again, a large part of the English contingent were from Cheshire. He marched from Bergerac in a northerly direction, through the province of Périgord to Périgueux, where on the second day they spent the night. The following night they camped at Ramefort and on 10 August, Brantôme; they by-passed the castle of Quinsac, believing it too strong for them to take. On they went into the province of Limousin where, at Bellac, they rested for two days before moving off to La Ferté-Saint-Cyr, on the River Cher. Having taken that castle the Prince sent Chandos and Audley ahead to check on the roads and the countryside, '*lest they be ambushed*'. On one such occasion, when the two men were out on a mission, they came across a division of the French army whom they immediately engaged and defeated; the prisoners they took informed the Prince that King John of France was near by with a large army intent on battle. The army moved on along the valley of the Cher towards Tours and on the way a party of French attacked the rear-guard but were soon put to flight. Prince Edward no doubt expected to see something of his cousin Lancaster in the area around Tours but there was no sign. The Prince embarked on chasing the small French band that had attacked him as far as the castle of Romorantin, where they took refuge. Chandos was sent to the castle to request the French to yield but they refused, so the Prince set about taking the castle by force. Froissart tells the story thus:

> *... The next day every man was armed under his banner and beganne to assayle the castell right feersly and the archers were on the dykes, and shotte so wholly togyder, that none durst scant apere at their defences. Some swame over dykes on bordes and other thynges, with hokes and pikes in their handes, and myned at walles and they within cast downe great stones and potts with lyme ...... The assault dured the day without rest, at night the englysshmen drewe to thie lognes and so past the nygt; in the mornyng, when the sonne was rysen the marshals of the hoost sowned the trumpettes. Then all such as were ordayned to gyve the assault were redy appayerelled, at the whiche assault the prince was personally, and by reason of his presence greatly encouraged the englysshmen...*

After five days the castle fell, having been set on fire with the use of 'greek fire'; its defenders fled and their leader and the other knights became the Prince's prisoners. Whilst one might think it foolish to linger in taking the castle given that a large french army was close by, it did provided much booty and provisions and the prisoners were able to supply valuable intelligence as to the enemy positions. Most of all such an event helped to boost the army's morale.

On reaching the outskirts of Tours the Prince waited for Lancaster for four days but still there was no sign. On 11 September, the Prince decamped and headed south, with the King of France hard on his heels. As they marched home, the Prince had the bridges he crossed burned to delay the pursuing French. By 17 September the French had managed to get ahead and were waiting at Chauvigny, east of

Poitiers. The English took a detour around the town and headed for the small town of Poitiers where unknown to the Prince a part of the French army was garrisoned. A scouting party ventured towards the town and spotted the French; they turned and ran back to their camp hotly pursued by the French who were then ambushed. Realising that the French would now know his position Edward sought a place to give battle.

On Sunday, 18 September, the English army took up their position on a ridge at Nouaillé, eight miles Poitiers. Above the village of Nouaillé the ridge rose steeply, its wooded slopes rose to a height of around 100 feet above the village. From the summit the ridge sloped gently down towards the north-west. Some 500 yards down the slope there was a hedge stretching from the marshy grounds at the side of the river Noisson to open ground on a plateau which formed the end of the ridge. At the right-hand end of the hedge the Prince had the waggon-train drawn up. From the hedge the slope ran down into a gully and then rose again up to a second ridge. This undulating countryside, cultivated for the growing of vines, was to be the scene of one of history's most famous battles.

The Prince placed his vanguard, under Warwick, to the left-hand end of the hedge: the rear-guard were placed at the other end under the Earls of Suffolk and Salisbury (their right being then protected by the waggons). The Prince's division arranged themselves further up the slope in a central position. The usual English recipe of trees, hedges. sloping ground, and the harrow deployment of men-at-arms and archers was again us used. During the day an interesting encounter took place which typifies the pride men took in their heraldic devices. Instead of using their coats of arms on their tunics some would wear a religious device. Sir John Chandos wore a white surcoat and on the breast he had had embroidered the Virgin Mary surrounded by the sun's rays. As he was supervising the formation of the English lines he was spotted by one of the French Marshals, Clermont. He bore on his breast a similar design and so he shouted, 'Chandos since when have you taken it upon yourself to wear my device?' Chandos replied, 'It is you who are wearing mine at least it is as much mine as yours'. The matter of right was soon to be resolved. The French, who numbered around 15,000 occupied the slope opposite the English. At dawn on Monday, 16 September the Earl of Warwick led some of the baggage train across the river in case a hurried retreat should be necessary. The French on seeing Warwick's move and believing that he was fleeing prepared to attack. The

Prince then spoke to his men to inspire them to perform great deeds of valour. According to Froissart, Sir James Audley pleaded with the Prince that he might have a position at the front of the ranks:

> *... 'Sir I have served always truly my lorde your father and you also, and so shall do so as long as I lyve; I say this because I made onse a vow, that the first batayle that the Kynge, your father, or any of his chtyldren shulde be at, howe I would be one of the first setters on, or els to dye in the payne; therefore I requyre your grace, os a rewarde for any servyce that ever I did to the Kynge your father or you, that you woll gyve me permission to depart fro you, and settle myselfe there as I may acomplyshe my vowe...'*

The Prince shook Audley's hand and granted his request, saying: '*... Sir James, God gyve you this day that grace to be the best knight of all others...*'. The Prince the apparently spoke to the archers, in the following way:

> *... 'Your courage and loyalty, have been well proved to me. In many, wild times you have shown that you are not degenerate Englishmen but flesh of their flesh and bone of their bone, who under the lead of my father, and my ancestors, Kings of England, found no task unconquerable..... Moreover, honour, love of country and the rich spoils of France, more than any words of mine, exhort you to tread in your father's steps. Follow your banners, keep your bodies and your wits intent upon the orders of your officers, so that if life and victory come, hand in hand, we may long maintain our fellowship, one in mind and in will...'*

The details of the battle have been well recorded by many eminent historians, suffice here to give a précis of the event. It was around mid-day when the French attempted to attack the strongly defended 'English' ridge. Apart from 300 men-at-arms the French fought on foot, an unpopular decision for the nobility of France, who believed that only peasants fought that way. King John's army was split into four: the cavalry led by the Constable of France and the two marshals Clermont and D'Audrehem; a division of foot led by the Dauphin, Charles; a second battle of foot led by the Duke of Orleans: and finally the King's division, the largest of all.

In the hedge there were two gaps through which two paths ran - one to Poitiers and one to the river. The initial attack came from the cavalry who had split into two divisions, each taking a gap in the hedgerow. Clermont took the gap which carried the road to Poitiers and managed to get through the defence despite heavy archery fire, whilst Audrehem was kept from getting through his gap. Seeing his colleague's difficulty Clermont wheeled to his right to attack Warwick, but as he did so Salisbury's men-at-arms successfully intercepted him and with the Prince's men were put to flight and Clermont killed. The Constable of France was also killed in this initial action. As the cavalry left the field the Dauphin's army of foot advanced. In heavy armour they trudged down from the ridge and up to the hedge. Unused to marching they soon grew weary and lost their necessary cohesion, becoming not much more than a tired rabble. The bravery of the French men-at-arms was such that they kept going and on reaching the English lines where fierce hand-to-hand fighting took place. Despite their large numbers the Dauphin's men were pushed back down the slope. Seeing their plight, the Duke of Orleans ran from the field taking with him nearly a quarter of the French army.

For a time the English were able to draw breath, and to sort themselves out before the French king's division appeared. On seeing their size many on the English thought that they would be defeated so, in an effort to boost morale, Edward ordered his men to mount and attack the enemy. The initiative worked. The army became excited at the prospect of advancing to meet the enemy instead of waiting for them. The French who were on foot now felt at a loss against a mounted charge. The Captal de Buch's division of the Prince's division had not seen action thus far and now they were ordered to ride under cover around the end of the 'English' ridge and to attack the advancing French in their left and rear. As the French reached the gully the Prince gave the order to charge. The Chivalry of England charged down the slope and crashed into the French and hacked their way through. Then the Captal de Buch appeared from around the ridge and charged into the rear of the French, causing havoc. The battle was won. As the battle drew to a close the Prince sent Warwick and Suffolk to find the French King. They eventually found him surrounded by men-at-arms eager for his capture. Warwick took the King of France to the Prince of Wales: the ultimate token of victory. What of Sir James Audley who served in the front line? Froissart continues the story:

> *...Asoone as therle of Warwyke, and the lorde of Cobhom were departed fro the prince, as ye hove herd before...... then the*

prince demanded of the knightes that wre aboute hym for the lorde Audeley yf any knewe any thyng of hym".

The Prince was informed that the valiant knight lay injured under a hedge so he sent some knights to collect him. Audley was informed that the Prince desired to see him so eight of his servants bore him in a litter to the Prince's tent. There the Prince took the knight in his arms and kissed him and called him the most valiant of knights. The Prince rewarded Sir James with a sum of 500 marks a year for life. Sir James was taken back to his lodgings where he told his squires and knightly colleagues what had been said to him. In the presence of his brother Sir Peter Audley, and other knights, he awarded the money due to him from the Prince to his four squires. On hearing of this generosity the Prince then awarded a further 500 marks a year to Sir James (a mark was a unit of surrency worth two-thirds of a pound sterling).

The identity of the four squires has caused some discussion among historians. Who were they? The story I have used has come from Lord Berners' translation of Froissart's chronicles which is illustrated with the arms of the squires and from these, tradition has given the names of Thomas Dutton of Dutton, John Haukestone of Wrynehill, John Delves of Doddington, and Robert Fouleshurst of Edlaston - four Cheshire men. The arms of the four families do have a similarity which is said to originate from this event. Sir James bore, 'Gules, fretty, Or' and the charge of a 'fret' or the use of a fretwork pattern is to be found in each case. The family of Dutton bore '*Quarterly, Argent and Gules; in the second and third quarters a fret, Or*'; Haukestone bore, '*Ermine, a fesse gules, fretty, Or*'; Delves bore, '*Argent, a chevron gules, fretty, Or, between three delves, Sable*'; and Fouleshurst bore, '*Gules, fretty, Or, on a chief Argent, two mullets Sable*'. However, the similarity of the charges on the shields cannot be taken as indicative of these men as being the four esquires or even of their presence at Poitiers with Sir James.

The family of Dutton had borne '*a fret, Or*' since at least the thirteenth century; in fact a seal of that period, inscribed Hugh de Dutton, clearly shows 'a fret'. The family of Despenser, an early offspring of the Duttons, bore the Dutton coat differenced by a 'bend, Sable'. Thomas Dutton was Sheriff of Cheshire at the time and it is not known for certain whether he was on the campaign – in any event it is unlikely he would have been serving Audley as a squire. It may be that Haukestone bore the similar charge to show that he was a tenant of the Audley family. As to John Haukestone, he was in the Queen's service and is unlikely to have been on the campaign. John Delves was not at the battle: he was lieutenant to Bartholemew de Burgersh, the Justiciar of Chester, and as such may have been fully employed in the county as the Justice was on the campaign. Fouleshurst certainly had letters of protection dated 28 June 1355 when going on the King's war but they do not say he was to join the Prince, though he could have joined the Prince in the spring of 1356. It should be noted that the family of Cheney of Nantwich bore, 'a bend, fretty, or' although a member of that family was at the battle it has not been suggested he was with Sir James; in fact the family may have used the pattern to show a marriage alliance with the Audley family.

The legend of Dutton, Delves, Fouleshurst and Haukestone must be treated with care, though I have no doubt that his squires were Cheshire men. Hewitt states that one of them was named Welles, a member of a Nantwich family.

On Tuesday 20 September, the victorious army and their prisoners set off for Bordeaux stopping at Libourne for a few days. They entered the city in the middle of October amid great rejoicing. Throughout the winter negotiations with France produced an agreeable peace treaty and in March 1357 the Treaty of Bordeaux was signed - there would be peace until Easter 1359 and the Prince and his army could now return home. On 24 May, the Prince and his illustrious prisoner entered London to a tremendous reception. He and his men were the heroes of the 'Age of Chivalry'; their exploits were told in ballad and song all over Europe.

* * *

What of Knolles and Lancaster? How had they fared in northern France? Why had they not joined the Prince in the Loire valley?

Having arrived back at Montebourg on the Contentin peninsula Lancaster began to plan his expedition to Brittany - his original intention. As the King's Lieutenant of the duchy, he and the young de Montfort had business to attend to. From Normandy Lancaster journeyed to Vannes by way of the coastal region of Penthièvre, arriving by 12 August. Whilst at Vannes he heard that Charles de Blois, the rival claimant to the duchy, had been released from captivity in England. De Blois had taken residence at Gaingamp in the north of the duchy and his presence there could not be tolerated.

Lancaster therefore marched north to retake the area around the town which forced de Blois to flee south to Nantes.

From Montebourg, Robert Knolles went to the castle of Fougères and from there set out to lay siege to the castle at Domfront held by Franco-Breton forces. Whilst busy on the siege Sir Robert heard that the Prince of Wales had reached the Loire valley and was heading for Tours so he abandoned the siege and headed for the Loire. Henry Lancaster also heard of the Prince's advance and likewise moved south to meet the Prince. Sir Robert and his force would have arrived in the Loire valley within a few days and may have made contact with the Prince's scouts. Lancaster had twice the distance to travel, and by the time he arrived at Pont de Cé he found that a large French army was barring his way and had to return. Sir Robert seems not to have remained with the Prince's army and in fact to have returned to the siege at Domfront.

Jointly, Robert and Duke Henry took many castles in or on the borders of Maine, Normandy and Brittany, effectively cutting Brittany off from the rest of France. They took and garrisoned such castles as Villiers, Bois-du-Maine, Messei, Tinchebray, St. Germain, Condé-sur-Noireau, Martainville, Saint James-de-Beuvron, Avranches and Domfront.

On 3 October, Lancaster laid siege to the large town of Rennes but the task was to prove difficult for the small army did not possess any machinery for a full siege. Throughout the winter the siege went on whilst Bertram du Guesclin and his forces harassed the besiegers. Early in 1357 Charles, Dauphin of France and Duke of Normandy, sent two forces to attempt to relieve the town. The first force was entirely defeated by Lancaster whilst the second, camped at Dinan thirty miles north, set about harassing the English. The degree of harassment was such that Henry decided to lay siege to Dinan and successfully took it.

The siege of Rennes then continued until the summer when Henry was ordered to give up due to the peace which then existed by the Treaty of Bordeaux. Lancaster, however, did obtain the city's surrender and was paid 100,000 crowns by its people. On 5 July Henry of Lancaster and ten of his knights entered the town and placed his banner on the walls. Du Guesclin offered the victorious commander a drink and then formally retired from the siege. Robert Knolles was present at the siege during the spring and early summer, after which Lancaster returned home leaving Robert to look after the Duchy of Brittany in his absence.

* * *

References for Chapter Three

Much of the material has come from the *Black Prince's Register*, Vol. III, especially as to recruitment. Details of payments made at Bordeaux may be found in the *Queen's Remembrancer* in the Public Record Office. Details of the accounts of the campaigns and the battle of Poitiers have come from many sources including the contemporary sources of Froissart and Le Baker. For details of the campaigns *The Crécy War* by Burne should be consulted, or *The Black Prince* by Emerson. Again, Sumption's *Trial by Battle: The Hundred Years War, Volume 1* (1999) and *Trial by Fire: The Hundred Years War, Volume 2* (2001) should be consulted.

***

AUDLEY
DUTTON
FOULESHURST
DELVES
HAWKESTON
CHENEY

4. THE COMPANIES

The Treaty of Bordeaux signed on 23 March 1357 by the Prince of Wales and King John, brought a formal peace. By the Treaty, King Edward was to be recognised as sovereign of Guînes, Montreuil, Ponthieu, Aquitaine and Calais; John II was to remain a prisoner until a ransom of 4,000,000 crowns had been paid. After the return of the victorious army Prince Edward set about rewarding his troops. To his commanders he gave sums of money, annuities and gifts of land; to his men-at-arms similar gifts; and to his archers, money, plots of land, agricultural rights and minor official posts. Some received pardons for wrongs committed before the campaigns. There is little doubt that some of the Cheshire people were well rewarded for their loyal service.

On 13 July, Sir Thomas Daniers received a general pardon for all felonies and trespasses committed in the County prior to 3 April 1357, but excepting the death of the Prince's ministers, Bartholemew de Norden and Richard Bechyngton. These ministers were slain in the County whilst on the Prince's business and their murderers had not been found, consequently the offence was exempted from the pardons. Danier's pardon states that it was granted on account of his 'good service in Gascony and especially at the battle of Poiters'; this pardon was followed on 1 July with a pardon for a fine of twenty marks then outstanding. Sir Alan Cheyne, who was knighted during the second *chevauchée*, having left England in August 1355 as the 'prince's yeoman', received an annuity of £40 for life by virtue of an order dated 1 February 1357. The order styles him 'prince's bachelor' suggesting his elevation to knighthood whilst in France and reads:

> *...in consideration of good services in Gascony and especially on account of the very good position he held on the day of the battle of Poitiers, when he was appointed to be in attendance on the Prince's person...*

On 16 November 1356 Sir John Chandos was granted the manor of Drakelow, near Northwich, for life, with an annuity of £40 from the rent of the Prince's tenants on Rudheath, Cheshire. Again, the reward was on account of his services at Poitiers, and in Gascony. William Golbourne was granted three oaks from the woods at Peckforton on 9 September and this was followed by a monetary award for his 'great labours', at the battle. Sir John de Hide, Sir John

Fitoun and John son of Henry Fitoun (Fytton) were all rewarded with pardons of all offences committed prior to 8 May 1357; again with exception of the killing of the Prince's ministers: the pardon was dated 19 July 1357. Richard Baskervylle of Withington received a lump sum of 100 marks for his services. Adam de Acton was granted the 'bailiwick of the Sergeanty of Bucklow'; Robert son of Piers Astelle was pardoned for the murder of John le Koo of Knutsford. William de Bollyngton was pardoned on 8 November 1356 for taking a doe in Macclesfield Forest. For his services Hamon de Mascy was exempted from jury service and Adam de Bostok was granted a pardon for his services.

In July 1357, it was mentioned that Thomas Gamul, John de Twembrok and his brother took part in the battle and there took a prisoner whose ransom was worth forty marks. Gamul alleged that he had not received his share of the ransom and that the two brothers had not given their halves to the Prince as was the custom. In the same month, John Fairchild and Benet le Wode quarrelled over their shares of a ransom. From the evidence given in the various rewards it is possible to produce a long list of people who served in Gascony and at the famous battle, but any list will by no means be complete as many grants may have been lost and there are perhaps many who were not rewarded. Many men did not return home with the army but preferred to stay and garrison some of the places captured from the French, whilst others formed themselves into armed bands living off the countryside of France.

* * *

The truce brought unemployment to many professional soldiers who, so accustomed to war, refused to accept the peace; maybe they believed that as other truces had failed, this one would do so too. The professional soldier was greedy for the profit of war - booty and ransom - peace would not supply that. The disgruntled unemployed warriors remained in France and formed themselves into gangs, offering their services to whoever would give them employment, or else they raided the country to sustain themselves. These marauding gangs or bands known as the 'Free Companies' caused some embarrassment to the truce and earned royal displeasure.

With the King of France a prisoner in England the country was ruled by the Dauphin and senior lords: the country was on the brink of civil war - the peasants were rising against the nobility of France and Charles of Navarre had decided to settle old scores in Normandy. Consequently, there was no shortage of work for free-booters. Of the many 'Companies', those led by Robert Knolles, Hugh Calveley, and Sir John Hawkwood (a man from Essex) are the most well known and the most documented. Another company was led by Sir John Griffin, or Griffith, who may, or may not, be the John Griffin of Barterton, near Nantwich. These 'Free Companies' were not peculiar to Englishmen as Gascons, Germans and Flemings formed similar groups. Roger Vercel, in writing of the life of Bertram du Guesclin, said of the 'handsome brutal soldiers' who formed the 'companies':

> *... if they have terrified people and history it is because they were in every sense of the word men of war. They practised war with a terrible sincerity. They divested it of all it's vain glory; they displayed it in it's frightful reality in it's beastial nudity. They had the only qualities that war requires, bravery and discipline... Their enemy was he who owned what they wanted. They pillaged with a fierce impudence in every camp. They did not trouble to themselves with excuses, they did not cloak themselves with flags or principles... As for other virtues that are held up to men of war magnanimity, respect of property and persons...the bandits rejected them either as nonsense or betrayal...*

The war fought on behalf of the King of Navarre was kept going largely by the acts of the English 'Companies'. Hugh Calveley having been released from captivity in 1355, stayed in northern France serving both the Brittany and Normandy causes. From 1355 until 1360 Hugh does not appear to have been so well known as his kinsman Robert; he had the patronage of the Duke of Lancaster, served him in the Normandy campaign and then seems to have served the King of Navarre there. By 1359, Hugh was the commander of Navarre's army so it would seem that he and his 'Company' had served Charles of Navarre well! The only known exploit of Hugh's at this time is in 1358 when he went to relieve the castle of Melun, where the Navarrois were holding the two dowager Queens of France as hostages, which was being besieged by French forces. Hugh and another Englishman, Sir James Pipe, put the French to flight.

Robert Knolles also served the King of Navarre for a time, though his main duties lay in Brittany. At the end of June 1357, together with the same Sir James Pipe, he defeated a French army before the port of Honfleur in Normandy. All through the following year Robert and his 'Great Company', as it was known, raided the country south of Paris; his skill as a warrior ensured abundant booty. On 2 May he took the castle of Chatillon-sur-Loing, and a little later made a flying raid through the province of Berry and into Auvergne, boasting that he would ride to Avignon and see the Pope: he actually managed to get within twelve leagues (thirty-six miles) of the Papal residence, causing great alarm. The French set out to stop him and at Clermont-en-Basse, in Auvergne, the Cheshire knight was opposed by a force of 10,000 men. Under the cover of night he withdrew and retired to Limousin, and eventually Bécheral in Brittany. A French chronicler says of Robert's activities:

> *...In the year of Our Lord 1358, the English came to Chantecocq, captured the castle and set fire to it and almost all of the countryside. Afterwards they brought the whole country under their rule, ordering all the owners of both great and small estates to pay ransome for their lives and goods and chattels, or their house would be burned...Roused and terrified many came to the English and agreed to buy themselves back, if they would cease for a little while their persecutions... Some they kept in unknown prisons threatening them every day with death and some they tortured unceasingly with scourgings and blows, hunger and dire want... Others having nothing with which to redeem themselves... made huts in the woods, there eating their bread in fear, sadness and grief... Among them I, Hugues de Montgeron, prior of Brailet in the parish of Domats... daily saw and heard of the base and horrible deeds of our enemies, of houses burnt and of many dead left lying about the villages and hamlets...*

In October 1358, Robert took the castles of Châteauneuf-sur-Loire and Malincorne. On 10 March in the following year he stormed the town of Auxerre; with him at the time was Thomas Fogg of Chester. This man is an interesting person: he seems to have been the Duke of Lancaster's captain of Domfront in Brittany in the 1350s and also had responsibility for garrisons at Villiers and Bois-de-Maine in the Mayenne valley. He went on to seize many castles from the French and even buy garrisons already held by his lord which he then placed under his own command, and earned himself a considerable sum of money during these years. The following month he ransomed the town for the sum of 50,000 moutons (one mouton equalled about four English shillings at that time). Early in 1359 he met up with

Phillip of Navarre and the Earl of Harcourt and they each then led a division to the relief of the town of St. Valéry-sur-Somme which the French had been besieging for many months. Knolles' pillaging in northern France was so terrible, that his routes were called 'Knolles' Mitres' from the appearance of charred gable ends of houses left behind. Froissart says of Sir Robert:

> *...on the sea coast of Normandy there were still a great number of English and Navarvois plunderers and robbers. Sir Robert Knolles was their leader who captured every town and castle he came to, there being none to oppose him. Sir Robert had followed his trade for some time and by it gained upwards of one hundred thousand crowns. He kept a great many soldiers in his pay; being very liberal he was cheerfully followed and obeyed...*

It is from about this time that sources style Sir Robert though exactly when he received the accolade is not known. In July 1359, he made an expedition along the Loire valley and took many castles and towns including the city of Orleans. In all Knolles made himself master of over forty castles in northern France. From the Loire he raided the country from Tonerre to Vezelay and from Nevers to Orleans. At Ancenis, on the Loire, the townspeople flung themselves into the river on hearing of the approach of Robert 'the terrible'. During this time its is said that Knolles declared that he fought for himself alone and did not serve the Kings of England or Navarre. He may not have served them directly but he certainly aided their causes - a useful ally. Sir Robert was said to bear the following legend on his banners:

Qui Robert Canolle prendera,
Cent mille moutons gagnera.

Although a brilliant commander he was on one occasion defeated. It was towards the end of September 1359 when he was captured in an ambush, though soon rescued by his friend Hannekin Francois. Later he served with Lancaster at the siege of Dinan where he endeavoured to arrange settle a quarrel between du Guesclin and Thomas de Canterbury. On his return to Brittany, Sir Robert sent word to King Edward that all the towns and castles which he had captured were at the King's disposal. Robert had obviously heard that his activities had upset Edward's political strategy and his offer was an attempt to appease him. It worked for Edward was delighted and rewarded Sir Robert with a pardon for his unofficial war and confirmed his possession of a number of the castles.

Sir Robert Knolles expedition during summer 1359.

* * *

References for Chapter Four

The details of rewards granted to Cheshire men may be found in *The Black Prince's Register*, Vol. III and the various Rolls of the period. The activities of Knolles have been taken from various sources: Barnes, *History of Edward III*; the *Chronicles of Jean le Bel*, the *Chronicles of Jean Froissart* (various editions); Walsingham's *Historle Anglicano*; and Knighton's *Chronicle*. Sir Arthur Conan Doyle's *The White Company* and *Sir Nigel* are fictional accounts of the Companies and Hubert Cole has written novels about Sir John Hawkwood, a Company commander. Whilst both authors make fictional references to Calveley and Knolles they are based on fact.

* * *

GOLBORNE

ARDERN

EGERTON

GOOSTREY

HASSALL

GAMUL

5. THE REIMS CAMPAIGN

It was in January 1359 when Edward III reaffirmed his claim to the Crown of France. The truce which had been signed at Bordeaux was to expire at Easter (21 April) but its terms had not been concluded - not even the first instalment of King John's huge ransom had been paid and France was in no position to conclude the terms for she had severe domestic problems. The peasants of northern France were in revolt against the Dauphin and his caretaker government, the country was plagued by the 'Free Companies', and Charles of Navarre was still waging his 'war'.

France's king in custody at Somerton Castle was in a dilemma. He offered the cession of Poitou, Anjou, Boulogne, Maine, Touraine and Normandy, in addition to those areas granted in the Treaty of Bordeaux. In return Edward agreed that the ransom of 4,000,000 crowns should be effectively reduced to cover all the nobles of France who were then in custody in England. The Treaty of London was signed on 24 March 1359 and sent to Paris for approval. The Dauphin, as expected, turned it down and realising the consequences of their rejection set about preparing for war. The Dauphin made a treaty with Charles of Navarre to prevent further hostilities until the English threat was over. Edward, King of England and 'of France', stated to all that he intended to march to Reims where he would be crowned King of France, 'and not return again until he had made an end of his war or else a sufficient peace to his great honour and profit'. Once again the King and his son Edward issued their orders for war; this time the two greatest generals of Europe were to assemble the largest army ever to have left the shores of England. The admirals were ordered to seize all shipping to ferry the army across to France - nearly 1,100 vessels were collected off Sandwich for the purpose.

Orders to array men and provisions were sent around the country and once again the county of Chester was required to produce men-at-arms and archers for the coming invasion. A thousand sheaves of arrows (a sheaf usually contained twenty-four) and 3,000 bow strings were ordered on 10 June, with an instruction that they should be ready by St. James' Day (25 July). On 28 June, the following command was sent to the Chamberlain of Chester:

> *...to buy sufficient green and white cloth for short coats and hats for the four hundred archers who have been chosen, tested and*

arrayed to go with the prince to the war, and to deliver the same to them in such manner as has theretofore been done, and to see that the one thousand sheaves o/ arrows and three thousand bowstrings are to be in readiness as ordered...

A similar instruction was sent to the Chamberlain of North Wales for fifty Welshmen who had been chosen. At the same time the knights, esquires and other men-at-arms were ordered to be at the Prince's manor of Northbourne, near Sandwich, Kent, by the Feast of the Assumption (15 August) without fail. The Cheshire auditors were to be in London by 'St. Peter's Chains, or within three days without fail' (1 - 4 August). The fifty Welshmen were probably from Flint for they were to wear the same uniform as the men from Cheshire; ten of them were to be armed with a lance and the rest with bows and arrows. It is unfortunate that the Black Prince's register for Wales is missing as the recruitment in Wales cannot be assessed properly. In August, the Prince moved from London to Northbourne to meet his troops. From his manor the Prince issued orders to the Chamberlain of Chester respecting the payments of the archers and their captains. The war fees quoted below are for half a year, though the men were in fact retained from he beginning of August for one year. Each knight received £10 for half a year and for each squire in his company five marks (£3 6s 8d). The order dated 16 August reads:

...pay the following sums to the under-mentioned bachelors of the prince, whom the prince has retained for the war for a year from St. Peter's Chains last, as their fees for half a year, to wit:
Sir John Danyel, with four esquires, £23 6s 8d.
Sir John de Hide, with two esquires, £16 13s 4d.
Sir John Griffyn, with one esquire, £13 6s 8d.
Sir John Fitoun, with one esquire, £13 6s 8d.
Sir Geoffrey de Wereberton, with two esquires, £16. 13s. 4d.
Sir William de Caryngton, with three esquires, £20.
Sir Ralph de Modberlegh, with two esquires, £16 13s 4d.
Sir William de Golbourne, with two esquires, £16 13s 4d.
Orders, also, to pay to the under-mentioned yeomen of the prince the following sums as their war-fees for half a year, to wit:
Thomas de Dutton for himself
and his two companions £13. 6s. 8d.
Hamon de Mascy, 5 marks
Richard de Mascy, 5 marks
Thomas de Stathum, 5 marks

Robert de Legh, 5 marks
William de Legh, 5 rnarks.
As regards the wages of the said knights and their esquires and of the said esquires (yeomen) of the prince. the prince orders that for the seven days journey to Northbourne each of the knights be paid 2s. a day and each of the esquires 12d. a day...beyond the seas with the prince, the prince orders that for the said seven days journey 6d. a day, for each archer to be paid to the leaders of the archers...

The Cheshire contingent arrived at Northbourne during the first few days of October; they must have been a marvelous sight, four hundred men all dressed in their green and white tunics and hats, following their banners displaying the heraldry of their commanders. The tunics were divided, as was the custom, with the green to the right. Green and white were the livery colours of the royal house of Plantagenet. The knights and men-at-arms would perhaps have been wearing tunics with their own heraldic devices.

Many archers fell ill on the journey south, and by the time they reached Kent they were too ill to continue abroad; once their captain had certified them too ill to travel they were allowed to return home, for example: Philip Filkyn, one of the prince's archers, was allowed to remain at home as Thomas Stathum, his leader, had testified that he was 'very feeble, and so burdened with illness', that he could not travel. On 1 October, Thomas de Blackenden and John de Swetenham, two archers who were to have joined Sir John de Wengefeld, pleaded that they had enemies amongst the archers who would kill them, and they therefore wished to stay at home. Similarly, John Clerc de Brudelegh, a servant to the Abbott of Combermere, feared for his life having enemies in the ranks and was allowed to stay at home. Richard de Clayford, bailiff and proctor to the parson of Macclesfield, was allowed to stay at home because of his need in the parish.

At the end of October, the army left England for Calais; an advance guard under the Duke of Lancaster had already left at the beginning of the month. On his arrival in Calais, the Duke met up with a large contingent from Germany, and whilst waiting for the main body of the army he raided the surrounding area. The Earl of March also set off early and raided the sea coast around Calais.

On 26 October, the King with his son and the huge army landed at Calais, where they remained for eight days whilst they collected themselves together. The army finally consisted of Englishmen,

Flemings, Hainaulters, Brabancans, Germans, and renegade Frenchmen. It was an unusual occurrence for a mediaeval army to begin a campaign in the autumn, with every intention of continuing through the winter; consequently more provisions than usual were required and 6,000 carts were required for transport.

On 4 November, the large feudal host marched out of Calais for Reims. 'It was a joy to behold them' wrote Froissart. Amongst the host there rode some of the original Knights of the Garter, that most ancient and honourable order of chivalry founded by Edward III in 1347. They included the Prince of Wales, Henry of Lancaster, the Earls of Warwick, Stafford, Salisbury, and March, Lord Burghersh, Lord Grey, Sir John Chandos and Sir James Audley. At the other end of the scale the army included smiths, carpenters, cooks, tailors, pages and falconers, (for the King meant to have his pleasure hunting).

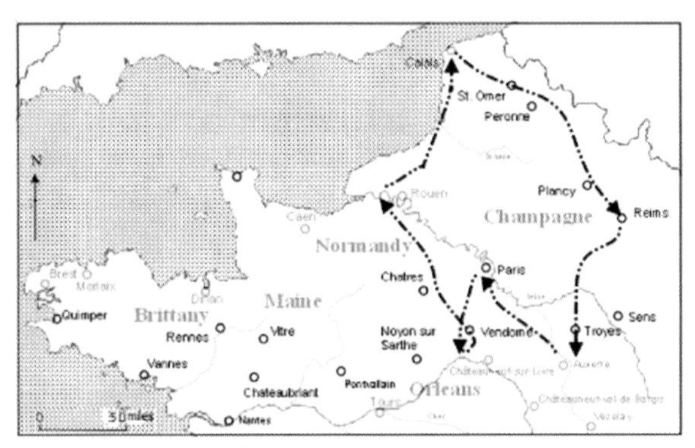

The Reims Campaign

The army was split into three battles. First, King Edward, with a total of 3,000 men-at-arms and 5,000 archers, accompanied by the Constable, William de Bohun, with 500 men-at-arms and a 1,000 archers - they formed the vanguard. Second, the Duke of Lancaster, with 600 men-at-arms. The rear-guard was commanded by the Prince of Wales with his brothers and 2,500 men-at-arms, and 4,000 archers. Among the Prince's division there rode a knight called Sir Thomas Grey, whose work *Scalonicra* gives an account of the campaign, and says of the Prince's battle, 'they rode at a soft pace ready ranged in battle as though they should incontinent have fought'.

Each of the three battles took a different route to Reims, spread out on a wide front. King Edward marched by way of St. Omer and

Champagne. Lancaster went by way of Agincourt, St. Pol, and Péronne. The Prince of Wales went on the longest route, by way of Montreuil, Hesdin and through Picardy, across the River Somme, to Nesle and Ham and into Vermondois, where they suffered a night attack on the quarters of the Earl of Stafford. The attack by French knights and arbalesters was easily repulsed and prisoners were taken. The following day they marched on to Saint-Quentin, and Château Porcien, finally reaching Reims and camping at Ville-Dommange, five miles south-west of the city. Edward had chosen to go to Reims as it was the traditional place for the crowning of the Kings of France and that the Archbishop of Reims was sympathetic to Edward's cause. However, by the time Edward arrived at the city, the Archbishop had changed his opinion.

It was 4 December when King Edward made his headquarters at the Benedictine Abbey of St. Basle, ten miles south of Reims. The weather throughout the journey had been atrocious 'the season was sore raining and wet, which did them great trouble, and their horses also' Froissart recorded. The army was wet and depressed, and to add to that the Archbishop kept the gates barred to them. The city was prepared for a long siege; they had had plenty of time to prepare as Edward had announced his intentions some time previously. Repeated demands were made at the gates, but they remained closed.

Whilst engaged on the siege the invading army amused themselves by raiding the surrounding territory. Lancaster raided the Ardennes, with the Earls of Richmond and March and took the towns of Otrey and Semay on the river Aisne. A detachment of the King's retinue raided the suburbs of Paris, but could not tempt the Dauphin to fight. Part of the Prince's division led by de Burgersh, the Justiciar of Chester, went to the castle of Cormicy. According to Froissart they mined the castle under the keep so that it was supported only on props. Sir Bartholemew then invited the keeper of the castle to view the damage, who on seeing it surrendered the castle to the English. Gray in *Scalacronica* states that the keep was mined and 'thrown down'. At the invitation of the French, the Justiciar of Chester amused himself in a contest of arms outside the walls of Reims. The tournament, fought *à outrance* (to excess), resulted in the death of one Frenchman and the wounding of two others by lance point.

* * *

The companies who joined the King on his march to Reims included Sir Robert's. Just prior to joining the King he had scored a success against Bertram du Guesclin in having taken the rough Breton knight prisoner in a skirmish at Pas d'Evran. On the campaign Knolles and his company served in Burgundy, Brie, Champagne, and Dairres where they took the town of Châlons-en-Champagne with a night attack though driven back from the richest quarter by a band of locals defending the bridge over the River Marne.

One of the two Sir James Audleys, either the one of Helegh or the other of Stretton, set off with the King Edward, whilst the other arrived at Chalons with a company from his castle of Ferté-en-Brie, along with the Captal de Buch, a French nobleman who supported the English cause, who had come from Clermont to join the King.

On 11 January 1360, after refusing to mount an all out attack on the city, Edward withdrew 'because he would not travail nor hurt his people'. Half of his troops were in no position to attack due to cold and hunger as the whole area around the city had been wasted by the French prior to the English arrival. On Edward's withdrawal the Germans and other nationals left for home but his numbers were not greatly reduced as the 'Free Companies' had joined the host.

The army moved south to Burgundy in search of a warmer climate and food for both men and horses. Once again the three divisions went separate ways, although heading in the same general direction. The Prince headed for Ligny-le-Châtel, near Auxerre, where his army 'suffered more from the enemy than in any other part of the expedition hitherto'. Several knights and esquires were killed in their sleep and foraging parties were taken. Despite hostilities in the area the Prince settled there for Lent securing a little stability by having taken the city of Auxerre, which a few years earlier had suffered a visit by Sir Robert Knolles. The King stayed at Tonerre on the river Yonne through Lent.

Whilst the Prince was at Auxerre, five of his squires went to a corn mill not far from the town to obtain provisions. The five men were not dressed in armour, but did have their helmets and their shields, and had three archers to protect them. Whilst they were obtaining flour fifty fully armed French men-at-arms swooped down on the mill eager to capture a party of Englishmen. The five defeated the fifty and took eleven prisoners. Even the French hailed this episode, and called it the 'exploit of fifty against five'. Who were the five men-at-arms and the three archers? As the Prince's personal retinue amounted to seven bannerets, 136 knights, 143 esquires, and 900 hundred mounted archers; and of the archers at least half were Cheshire men, and of the men-at-arms a fair proportion were also Cheshire men, we may suppose that a Cheshire man may have figured in the exploit.

Edward succeeded in making a treaty with the Duke of Burgundy, which was to last for three years, in exchange for their paying 200,000 moutons d'or. On 15 March the whole army moved north in the general direction of Paris: the King went via Gatinais and the Prince by way of Moret. Close to the town of Moret there lay a castle called Villemaréchal which was occupied by one of the companies and under siege by the French, when the Prince approached the French withdrew.

On the way to Paris Edward learnt of a French raid on the English port of Winchelsea; a troop of 2,000 had sacked the town and killed several hundred people. As a consequence, the King ordered his army to sack and burn every village they came to as they hurried on towards Paris.

During March 1360, a French raiding party took the town of Honfleur from England's grasp. Sir Thomas Fogg, one of Knolles' lieutenants, hearing of the matter sallied out of a neighbouring castle which he was holding and retook the town. Finding the town low on supplies he went out foraging with a small company of men when all of a sudden his party came upon 200 French men-at-arms and 200 arbalesters; the English only numbered forty men-at-arms and 100 archers. Both sides dismounted and engaged one another; despite the odds the French were beaten and their two leaders were taken prisoner along with other French knights.

About the same time, James Audley and a company from the garrisons at Ferté and Nogent, attacked a small town near Soissons, which was well provisioned and full of 'gentle ladies'. A party of Welsh archers who were in the following of Lord Spencer were in Beauce (near Tours), looking after a number of corn millers from Bonneval, when they were seen by a French party from a nearby garrison. The French, who numbered twenty-six 'lances' (a lance consisted of one knight or man-at-arms with two or three colleagues) and twelve archers, attacked the eight Welsh archers who immediately dismounted and engaged their enemy 'smartly'. The French were defeated, three of their men-at-arms killed and nine made prisoner, 'every man on both sides being wounded near to death'.

On Tuesday 31 March, King Edward arrived near Paris and set up his headquarters at Chanteloup; the Prince camped at Corbeil, less than thirteen miles from the city. The Dauphin had the city suburbs burned to the ground to limit the cover available should the English army attempt to assault the city walls. On Good Friday peace talks were held but without result and after Easter the King moved his camp to Montrouge nearer to Paris. The Prince and his Cheshire men raided the area around the city including Gentilly, only three and a half miles from the Dauphin's residence in the city. Following another fruitless conference on 10 April, the Prince and Lancaster rode up to the walls of Paris and around the city all day setting various defences on fire. Whilst the Prince and Lancaster were thus engaged the main body of the army withdrew. Eventually the two commanders also withdrew, leaving a small rearguard in the suburbs. On seeing the small rearguard the French sallied out to take it but the English expected as much and an ambush had been prepared. The rearguard was formed of men-at-arms of the Prince's personal retinue, some of whom had been newly knighted. One of the new knights was Sir Richard Baskerville of Withington, a Cheshire man. During the encounter he was thrown from his horse but then sprang to his feet and began to fight off the French who surrounded him; eventually he was rescued by his colleagues and the French were driven back to Paris somewhat shaken. Who the other newly dubbed knights were can only be speculation, but Thomas Dutton was knighted in 1360; Hamon and Richard Mascy were dubbed between 1359 and 1361; and another to receive the accolade at this time was Robert Fouleshurst.

On the first day of the withdrawal from Paris, towards the region of Beauce, the weather was extreme: rain, hail, snow and thunder and terribly cold. The next day a severe thunderstorm occurred when the army were near to Gallardon, between the forest of Rambouillet and Chartres. Men and horses were sail to have been killed by lightning, 'such a storm and tempest that none of our nation heard nor saw never none such'.

During the retreat, a knight called Sir Brian Stapleton, and some other knights of the Prince's retinue, were protecting foragers when they were attacked by a large party of Frenchmen. In the skirmish the French were beaten off. Sir Brian may have been related to the family which settled near Macclesfield. He was a witness to an armorial dispute between John Mascy of Tatton and his namesake of

Potington. Two other witnesses were Sir Hugh Calveley and Ralph Stathum. Sir Brian was one of the standard bearers to the Prince.

Faced with the prospect of further devastation the Dauphin sent envoys to King Edward with offers of peace. The Duke of Lancaster urged the settlement and so the army moved back in a northerly direction to Sours, where the English headquarters were set up on Tuesday, 1 May, talks began in earnest at Brétigny, a village between Sours and Chartres: a week later agreement was reached.

By the Treaty of Brétigny, Edward once again renounced his claim to the French crown; he also renounced his claim to Normandy, Anjou, Maine, Touraine, Brittany and Flanders, and agreed to hand back the castles and towns taken in those areas. In return King Edward was to hold free from suzerainty Aquitaine, Gascony, Guienne, Poitou, Saintonge, Agennis, Rouergue, Ponthieu. Montreuil, Calais and Guines; 'in all freedom and perpetual liberty as sovereign lord and liege and as neighbour to the Kings and realm of France, without recognising the King or Crown of France as sovereign, nor paying any homage, obedience, appeal, subjection to him, nor in any future time rendering him any service or recognition'. France also agreed to pay 300,000 crowns (a crown equalling about 3s 9d) in instalments for the King's ransom. Payments were to begin on 24 June, on which date the King would be released. As security for the payments the King's younger sons would become hostages. Each side denied an alliance, France with Scotland, and England with Flanders. On 15 May, the Prince of Wales took an oath in the great minster at Louviers for his part in the Treaty. The English army then withdrew towards Le Neubourg, Picquigny, and finally Calais.

As a result of the treaty, Sir Thomas Fogg of Chester was ordered to supervise the withdrawal of troops from Chateauneauf-en-Thymerais, Ferté-Villeneuil, and Nogente-Rotrou; also Domfret, Messai, Condé-sur-Sarthe, and the town of Villiers. Before finishing his task he was able to extract 20,000 ecus d'or (pieces of gold) from the people of northern France.

Once the Peace Treaty had been drawn up Sir Robert Knolles retired to Brittany to continue the struggle between the rival partisans for the Duchy. On 1 April 1360, a promise of safe conduct was granted to his wife Constance on her leaving England to join him in Brittany. She had with her an escort of twenty men-at-arms and forty mounted archers. Constance was a member of the Yorkshire family of Beverley and Leyland says she was 'a woman of mene birth and sometime of a dissolute lyvyng before mariage' and that she was a native of Pontefract.

* * *

References for Chapter Five

Much of the material has been taken from Sir Thomas Gray's *Scalacronica*. Froissart has again been used, and the two account for the accounts of the campaign. *The Black Princes Register* has again been used for details of recruitment. The description of Knolles' wife comes from Leyland's *Itinery*, vol. i.

FOGG

WETTENHALL

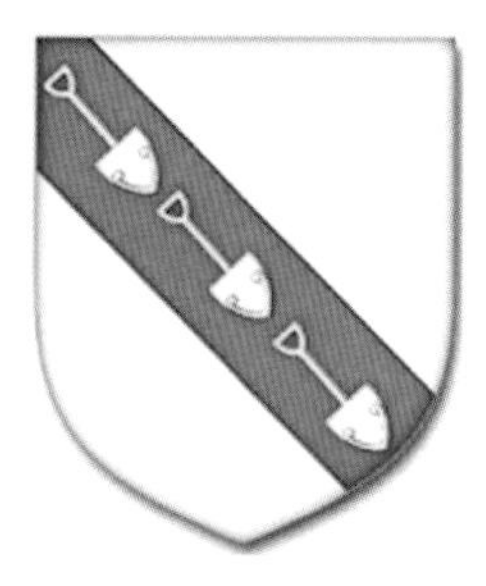

SWETTENHAM

DODD

CREWE

FITTON

6. COMPANIES AND CASTILE

In December 1360, Sir Thomas Holland, Earl of Kent, died. He had been the most chivalric knight of his day, and a founder member of the Order of the Garter founded in honour of Joan, Holland's wife, who it is thought had had an affair with the King. She was an attractive woman and her marriage to Holland was her third; her critics said she was promiscuous. Following Holland's death she won the heart of Edward, Prince of Wales, and on 10 October 1361 they married much to the embarrassment of the court.

In July 1362 Prince Edward was appointed Prince of Aquitaine and given sovereign rights in south-west France and twelve months later he embarked on a journey to his Principality, taking his wife with him. The Prince took a number of troops to garrison his castles and some of these were Cheshire men. The men of the county had been travelling between England and Aquitaine for some years. In 1359 Richard son of Hugh Henhull, Thomas de Dutton, William son of John Trussell, and Howel ap Oweyn, travelled to France.

In 1362 and 1364, Sir John Daniers made the journey. In July 1362 orders were issued to John de Delves and John de Burnham, the two county administrators:

> *...to cause one hundred and sixty of the best archers they can find to be chosen tested and arrayed in the county of Cestre, without sparing anyone, so that they be ready to set forth with the prince by the feast of the Nativity of Our Lady (8 Sept.) at the latest. The Chamberlain is to cause them to be clothed in green and white as has been the custom...*

In February 1363, a further 200 archers were ordered:

> *...to be paid a month in advance and their leaders knights and esquires, to be paid a half year in advance...'*

Having been made Prince of Aquitaine Edward had authority to appoint his own officials; some of the key posts went to Cheshire men. Sir Thomas Wettenhall was made Seneschal of Rouergue; Sir Richard Baskervylle, Seneschal of Agenais; Sir Thomas Felton, thought to have been a Cheshire men, Seneschal of Aquitaine, his cousin Sir William Felton, Seneschal of Poitou. David Craddock, of

Weston, near Nantwich, was appointed to the mayoralty of Bordeaux, having served as deputy to Wettenhall. Sir John Chandos, (who held much land in Cheshire and such appointments in the shire as 'Keeper of the Forest of Macclesfield), was made High Constable of the Principality. Another Cheshire man who was active at this time was James Mascy the captain of Millau castle. Of these men, it is worth mentioning Sir Thomas Wettenhall. He was a skilful administrator who operated from a base at Villefranche who came to a disastrous end. Whilst based in Rouergue he was accused by the French of having imprisoned and killed two of their ambassadors who had taken papers to the Prince of Wales in 1368: the accusation was probably false as Wettenhall had been in England during 1367-688 only returning at Christmas 1368. Unfortunately, he was captured in a skirmish in 1369 and sent to Toulouse where he was imprisoned for a year before being hung from a high scaffold specially built in the town square.

Although matters in Aquitaine were somewhat quiet, the same can not be said of northern France, where Sir Hugh Calveley and his kinsman, Sir Robert Knolles, were active. A condition of the Treaty of Brétigny, had been the withdrawal of the 'Free Companies'. Despite the various nationalities King Edward was held responsible for their activities and they were considered by the French as part of England's 'war machine'. It was no easy task for Edward to recall these mercenary bands for they were their own men, and owed him no allegiance; those who did owe Edward allegiance did return.

Charles of Navarre who held important castles in Normandy, as brother-in-law to the Dauphin, continued his arguments against the King of France; he continued to raid Normandy and intrigue with the Prince of Wales. The Captal de Buch became Charles' lieutenant, and as such he joined a freelance company of Navarrois plunderers led by an Englishman called John Jewel.

At Easter 1364, the Dauphin became King Charles V of France : his father had died a captive at the palace of Savoy. Charles now set about dealing with the threat posed by his brother-in-law's mercenaries and sent Bertram du Guesclin to Normandy with a large force. On 16 May Jewel's company met du Guesclin at Houlbec-Cocherel, a village between Evreux and Vernon; each side numbered around 2,000. The battle, which was one of the bloodiest of the time, was a victory for the Breton knight as Jewel was killed and the Captal de Buch was taken prisoner.

In Brittany the rivalry between de Montfort and de Blois continued despite a clause in the Treaty of Brétigny, which stated that they should settle by arbitration. Throughout the decade du Guesclin continued to take towns and cities from the grasp of the companies in Maine, Normandy and Brittany. In 1360 he had been captured at Juigne-sur-Sarthe, but having been ransomed for 30,000 écus d'or, he continued his activities against the companies.

Early in 1361 Sir Robert Knolles returned to England, but by July he was back in Brittany having brought forty men-at-arms and eighty archers to garrison two castles Grand-Fougeray and Castleblanche; he had been granted the lease of the two castles by the King for a rent of 1,000 marks (£666). On 28 April 1363, a force of twenty men-at-arms and forty mounted archers left England to join Sir Robert; two months later he laid siege to Bécherel which eventually fell to him and became his base. Sir Robert then went on to ravage Auvergne, with Louis of Navarre; they plundered the Bourbonnais and all the country between the Loire and the Allier. Territory which Sir Robert had 'worked' in many times before. During 1362, 1363 and 1364 Sir Hugh Calveley continued to raid and pillage northern France, mainly in Normandy. In the latter year he was commanding the garrison at Le Pont d'Orme, when a force led by du Guesclin came upon him and besieged him. The siege lasted for many months before Calveley had to surrender. Once again Calveley became Bertram du Guesclin's prisoner, however, his ransom was soon paid.

* * *

The Prince of Wales decided to send Sir John Chandos to northern France to represent his interest in the activities of Calveley and Knolles for, despite the formal peace, du Guesclin was representing the King of France as well as Charles de Blois. In July 1365 de Montfort laid siege to the town and castle of Auray. The besieging army split into four divisions, numbered similarly: the vanguard under the command of Sir Robert Knolles and Sir Walter Hewitt; the second under Sir Oliver de Clisson; the next under John de Montfort; and the rear-guard under Sir Hugh Calveley. The overall command of the army was in the hands of Sir John Chandos. De Blois and du Guesclin set off with an army of 4,000 to relieve the siege. Sir Hugh, being the proud man he was, felt that to command the rearguard and to be held in reserve was beneath his dignity. When battle between the two forces was imminent Sir Hugh begged Chandos to give him another command. Calveley was so belligerent that Chandos, 'with tears in his eyes, and on bended knee', had difficulty in persuading Hugh to take the command he had been given; he pleaded with Sir Hugh, stating that such a position was a responsible one and that there was no better to take such a command.

The battle of Auray was fought on 29 September 1365. It was a fierce contest with both sides fighting on foot. Although the English archers opened the battle, they found that their arrows were not penetrating the French armour, which had in recent years been improved. The archers threw their bows down and joined the men-at-arms to fight with their swords. The archers, lightly clad, were able to run rings' around the French men-at-arms, snatching their weapons, and using them on their previous owners. On four occasions Sir Hugh's rearguard had to advance to strengthen weak points and to keep the army together. He ordered his men to remove their 'cuissarts' (armour protecting the upper leg) to enable them to move more nimbly. Sir Hugh's actions with the rear-guard helped to save the day, and bring victory to the English side. At the end of the day, de Blois lay dead, and du Geusclin was a prisoner. John de Montfort was left the undisputed Duke of Brittany. After the battle King Charles of France accepted the situation and Montfort's dukedom, upon condition that he did homage to the crown of France in return. A temporary peace was brought to northern France.

As a reward for his part in the Battle of Auray Sir Robert was given the towns and castles of Derval and Rouge, with 2,000 'livres de rente' from the lands in Conq, Brittany. With the advent of peace in Brittany Sir Robert went to his new possession, the castle of Derval, and there he made his home.

* * *

The next theatre of war in which our Cheshire heroes served was Spain which in the fourteenth century was split into five separate kingdoms, of which the Kingdom of Castile and Leon was the largest. Castile was surrounded by the other four: Granada, Portugal, Navarre, and Aragon. Each country had its own King, respectively Peter the Cruel, Mohammed, Peter the Severe (uncle to Peter the Cruel), Carlos the Bad and Peter. Peter the Cruel was the eldest son of King Alfonso XI and had a half brother Henry, Count of Trastamara, the eldest of many illegitimate children fathered by Alfonso. Henry had been born in 1333 and was twelve months older than Peter. Castile was on good terms with England, in fact her King had been betrothed to Joanna, daughter of Edward III; unfortunately she died on the journey to Spain in 1348. The King of England also had offered to educate the bastard children of Alfonso and his mistress Dona Leonora.

In 1354 attempts were made by the peers of Castile to oust Peter from the Kingdom and replace him with Henry. The church backed this decision as Peter was an excommunicate, and so did Peter of Aragon, who had no liking for his namesake. The initial rebellion was soon put down but it rose again with the added support of Navarre. The renewal of the civil war, and the later developments were to involve Sir Hugh Calveley, Sir Robert Knolles, and other unknown Cheshire men.

Charles V decided to delve into the affairs of Spain, and informed the Pope that he intended to support the Bastard's claim to the throne; he then conspired with Aragon and made a peace treaty with Navarre, thus solving one domestic problem. Charles next sent Bertram du Guesclin to parley with the leaders of the companies, and to offer them rewards for service in a combined operation against Peter. The mercenary bands agreed to join du Guesclin, and Charles found a ready-made army for service in Spain and had thereby solved another of his domestic problems. The wages of the army, it was agreed, would be paid by both France and the church. In May 1365, the Pope sent a request to Prince Edward that the large army might pass through Aquitaine on its way to Spain. Because of Edward's friendship with Castile, and in particular its rightful King, the Pope informed Edward that the army was embarking on a 'crusade' against the Moors in Granada. Edward was convinced and he granted protection to the 'crusade'. The large army crossed the Pyrenees into Spain: the Bretons were led by du Guesclin and the French by Marshal d'Audrehem with the English contingents being led by Sir Hugh Calveley. No doubt Sir Hugh felt obliged to join the campaign as he was still in the service of Carlos of Navarre, but Sir Robert Knolles had no such obligation, and perhaps knowing of the true cause he remained in Brittany at Derval.

Later in the year King Edward learnt of the true reason for the campaign, and he accordingly recalled his subjects. On 3 December, an edict was published forbidding Sir John Chandos, Sir Nicholas Dagworth, Sir William Elmham, and Sir Hugh Calveley from going to Spain; only Sir John obeyed the command. The others stated that they would continue but only for so long as their Sovereign should not require them.

By the end of the year the army began crossing into Spain, by way of Catalonia, from where officers of the King of Aragon's army guided them through to Castile. The marauding horde had no respect for person or property of friend or foe on their way through; burning and pillaging as they went. On 2 February 1366, the people of Barbastro fled in terror, some took refuge in the church but were burned alive; and they were the subjects of the King of Aragon!

On to Borja they marched, where Sir Hugh sacked the town, then along the River Ebro to Logrono and west via Nájera to Burgos in the heart of Castile. On Palm Sunday, 29 March 1366, Henry of Trastamara was crowned King of Castile and Leon at Burgos. As a reward for his services du Guesclin was created Count of Trastamara, Henry's old title; Sir Hugh Calveley was created Count of Carrion.

Just prior to Henry's crowning, Peter fled to Toledo and then Seville, in vain he tried to buy off Calveley and du Guesclin. The ordinary peoples of Castile offered little resistance to Henry's invaders, who in an effort to justify the 'crusade' slaughtered many Jews and Saracens, seizing their treasures to pay the soldiers. Sir Hugh had all such treasure sprinkled with Holy Water to cleanse it!

Finding no support at Toledo or Seville, Peter went to Portugal, his uncle's kingdom, but no sanctuary was offered for fear of reprisals; so on he went to the province of Galicia northern Spain, where he was finally offered protection and settled at Corunna.

Although Seville would not offer sanctuary to Peter, the people would not allow the invaders to enter her gates either. The city proved a difficult task for Sir Hugh and the new king remarked on Hugh's apparent inefficiency, which hurt his pride so he attacked the city again, and after six hours took part of it and hoisted his banner from one of the towers. Seeing the 'calves' flying from the city, du Guesclin attacked from the other side and the city was won.

Peter and Edward began to plan the recapture of the Kingdom of Castile. It was necessary for England to maintain a strong alliance with Castile and have a friendly King on the throne, for she possessed a strong fleet of galleys with which England's vital shipping could be protected. Castile was also a useful base for operations in southern France. By a Treaty dated 1362 the two countries were bound to one another; Edward had to help.

The road to Castile lay through the Kingdom of Navarre and it was decided to buy Carlos' support, which turned out to be an easy matter. By the treaty of Libourne, dated 23 September 1366, Carlos sided with Peter in return for the province of Gipuzkoa (which lay between Navarre and the Atlantic), the neighbouring province of Alava, all the castles on the Ebro from Haro to Alfaro, and 200,000 florins for himself. Navarre's troops were to be paid 30,000 florins a month.

With the alliance in place Edward recalled his subjects from Spain, to assemble with the Prince of Wales; he sent his second son John of Gaunt from England to Bordeaux with 700 men, of whom nearly a half were Cheshire archers. The Prince sent for Sir Robert Knolles to join him. On 10 January 1367, the Prince arrived at Dax to await the collection of his forces, a few days later his brother John arrived and after that some of the English forces from Castile.

Hearing that Carlos had gone back on their agreement, Prince Edward sent word to Sir Hugh Calveley, who was at Calahorra and ordered to invade Navarre and secure a route for the Prince. He advanced up the River Agra and took the towns of Miranda de Arga and Puento la Reina, effectively guarding the Prince's route to Castile.

From Pamplona the English army marched in three battles. The vanguard was led by John of Gaunt, the twenty-seven years old Duke of Lancaster (he had inherited the Duchy from his father-in-law Henry, who had died in 1360); the young Duke was assisted by Sir John Chandos. The main body of the army was led by the Prince; with him he had Peter and Carlos, who, because of Calveley's action, had seen the error of his ways. Sir Robert Knolles also rode with the Prince as did the prince's stepson Thomas Holland. The rearguard was led by Sir Hugh Calveley, John II de Grailly (the captal de Buch) and the King of Majorca, who had a personal score to settle with Henry's ally, Peter of Aragon.

Burgos was the first major town on the route. To reach it the army had a choice of routes, either by way of Vitória or by way of Logrono. Choosing the more southerly route, the Prince sent Sir WIlliam Felton to reconnoitre the road; he took with him a band of 200 men-at-arms and 200 mounted archers. Sir William duly reported back that Henry and his army were at Santo Domingo de la Calzanda, east of Burgos, on the Logroño road. Henry had under his command Bertram du Guesclin and Marshal d'Audrehem. The

Prince therefore marched to Vitória. Felton kept a watch on the Bastard's army and reported its eventual move towards Vitória.

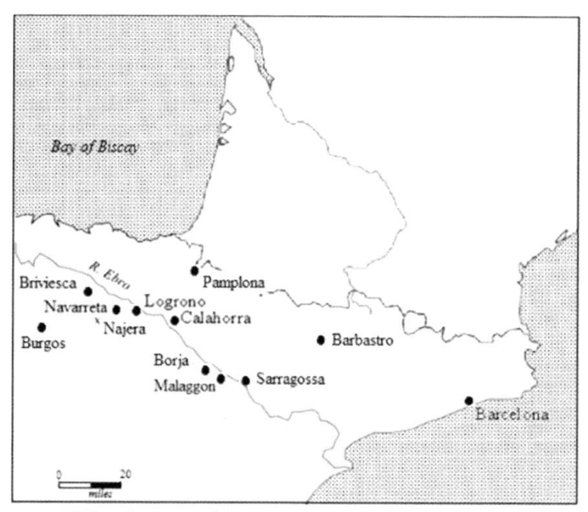

The theatre of operations in Northern Spain

Before moving to Vitória, Henry sent a raiding party forward, which made a dawn raid on Sir Hugh's camp, killing many of his men. As John of Gaunt rode to help, Tello (Henry's brother) and the raiders withdrew. They fell upon Felton who was marching to join the Prince. Felton found himself outnumbered fifteen to one, and took up a defensive position on a hill near Ainez, today known as 'Inglesmondi' (the hill of the English). It took Tello all day to defeat the small English army; in the end Felton and his men lay dead. The battle lasted all day due to the efforts of the English archers. But d'Audrehem had learnt the English tactics, and was able to overcome them eventually.

The Prince's army found itself bottled up outside Vitoria in a narrow gorge. On du Guesclin's advice, Henry made no move against them, intending to starve them out into retreat. On the night of 29 March, the Prince decamped and made to retreat then making a flanking manoeuvre through the mountains in a south-easterly direction emerging two days later near Logrono. For a week Henry had no idea where the Prince had gone, but on realising he had been tricked he decamped and made to cut him off. Henry arrived at the town of Nájera on 2 April and as he and Edward were now only several miles apart. Battle was inevitable.

Henry's army was split into two divisions; the vanguard led by Bertram and the Marshal, and a main body under the Castilian commanders: they numbered about 30,000.

Edward's army was much as it had been throughout the march. Lancaster and Chandos led the vanguard of around 3,000 men; the main body under the Prince amounting to 4,000 men; and the rear-guard under Sir Hugh giving a total of around 10,000. The main body was subdivided into a left wing under Sir Thomas Percy and Sir Walter Hewitt; a centre under the Prince and Peter; and a right wing under the Captal de Buch. Sir Robert Knolles and his men fought in Sir Walter Hewitt's company on the left wing. All except the rear-guard were to fight on foot.

Henry expected the Prince to attack along the Navarrete to Nájera road, however, under cover of darkness, Edward advanced behind a ridge, and over it to present himself on Henry's left. With the sudden sight of the English banners on his left Henry ordered his army to regroup to face their enemy. With this unexpected arrival of the English the Bastard's army became unnerved and some of his force deserted; some of his cavalry considered Edward's move such a bad omen for Henry that they deserted to Edward's side. Before Henry's army had been completely re-organised, belligerent du Guesclin commenced battle by charging the English vanguard; the battle of Nájera had started.

It was the morning of 3 April 1367. With the inital attack the archers commenced their usual deadly fire power, but it had little effect on du Guesclin's heavily armoured men. As the Prince and the main body of the English army charged down the ridge, Henry ordered his brother, in command of the left flank, to attack the right flank of the English vanguard. The archers concentrated their fire against Tello, because the Castillian infantry were clad only in chain mail; the hail of arrows produced by the English archers was extremely effective. Tello fled with his infantry, hotly pursued by the Captal de Buch, who, on seeing Tello's advance, had charged in support. Sir Walter Hewett was ordered to attack du Guesclin's right; the Count of Dinan rode to block him, but had little effect. Henry with his heavy cavalry rode forward; his horses, having little protection, were soon cut down by the English archers, causing the usual havoc of fallen horses and men. Henry withdrew. Three times he charged, three times he was sent back. After the fourth charge Henry fled, and was instantly pursued by Sir Hugh Calveley and the rear-guard, who until this time had seen little action. Henry's cavalry fled towards the fast flowing river Nájera where many were drowned, or put to the sword; the river ran red with the blood of men and horses. Many Castilians fled into the nearby town of Nájera where they were routed and slain. The battle was won.

Henry's losses were great and the English only slight. Two thousand were taken prisoner, including the notorious du Guesclin, and Marshal d'Audrehem. It was said that the battle had brought death to 16,000 men!

Great gallantry had been seen on each side. Sir John Chandos, who had captured du Guesclin single handed, was promoted to knight banneret; Peter himself cut the tails off Chandos' pennon. On one occasion Sir John had ridden ahead of his company and become surrounded by the enemy, one of whom plunged a dagger through his visor. Sir John managed to draw his own dagger, killed his opponent,'leapt to his feet, grasped his sword with both hands and plunged again into the melée, which was fierce and marvelous to watch.' In the true spirit of Chivalry, Sir Hugh paid du Guesclin's ransom to Sir John. Sir Hugh and Sir Bertram had pledged themselves brothers in arms to share the spoils of war. On his release he embraced Sir Hugh and went off to rejoin Henry.

One who could not be called gallant was Carlos of Navarre, who had himself conveniently 'captured' by one of the enemy and imprisoned at a castle on the border of Aragon and Navarre. After the battle he 'escaped', and then placed his gaoler into a dungeon to keep him quiet. Despite his not being present, his chamberlain and a number of his company were in the thick of the battle.

Henry and his wife and family fled to Aragon, so Peter sent Calveley, to whom he had re-granted the title of Count of Carrion, to the kingdom to demand Henry's extradition but was unsuccessful.

Having seen Peter reinstated on the throne of Castile and Leon, the Prince of Wales returned to Valladolid, to await his payment and reward from Peter. The promises of payment were broken, and all that the English troops got was dysentery and fever; disappointed, they withdrew to Aquitaine. The only thing that the Prince did receive was a large ruby, today known as the Black Prince's ruby, which is set in the Imperial Crown.

Sir Hugh Calveley and Sir Robert Knolles seem to have remained behind in Spain, for on 2 May Sir Robert was still at Burgos. Sir Hugh was commanded to remain to await any payments that might be made for the Prince. At the end of April, Hugh went to negotiate with Peter of Aragon to promote a triple alliance with Castile and

Navarre to prevent Henry rising again. Henry, however, successfully negotiated with the French Count of Anjou to assist him in retaking Castile, in return for assistance in his retaking parts of Aquitaine. Despite the triple alliance, Henry managed to retake the Kingdom by defeating Peter in a battle near Toledo. Peter flew to the castle of Monteil where he was found by du Guesclin and taken prisoner. The Breton knight then took him to King Henry who, by his own hand, killed him. The Spanish affair was over. Prince Edward had laboured in vain for eventually Castile became allied to France - against England.

*   *   *

References for Chapter Six

Much of the Chapter has come from Froissart and *Rymer's Foedera*. Sir Arthur Bryant's *Age of Chivalry*, has been referred too, as has *The Black Prince* by Emerson, and the work of the same name by Hubert Cole. The early references to recruitment have again come from either *The Black Prince's Register* or the various state rolls.

***

DOWNES

BASKERVILLE

MOBBERLEY

GROSVENOR

7. ROYAL COMMISSIONS

Edward's involvement with the ill-fated Peter of Castile heralded the downfall of England's hold of France in the fourteenth century. On 14 May, 1369, Charles V of France declared that all English property was forfeit and three weeks later King Edward met his Parliament and advised them that earlier peace treaties were invalid, and asked for financial aid and support in once more asserting himself King of France. In south-west France trouble was brewing: the Bishop of Toulouse was preaching rebellion in the province of Quercy; the towns of Cahors and Villeneuve-sur-Lot declared themselves for King Charles. Rebellion against the prince of Aquitaine had begun.

The Prince of Wales summoned Chandos from Saint-Sauveur le-Vicomte in Normandy; Knolles from Derval in Brittany and Sir James Audley from Fontenay-le- Comte. From England, Edmund Earl of Cambridge, brother to the Prince, and John Hastings, Earl of Pembroke, arrived to help the Principality of Aquitaine. Sir Robert received his summons in April 1369. He equipped a small force and embarked at Conq for Rochelle, and eventually joined the Prince at Angoulême, where he was holding court. Sir Robert's force numbered sixty men-at-arms and sixty archers.

From Cheshire a number of men answered the call to help; they included Sir Richard Fytton, John Gryffin, and Richard de Wynyngton as men-at-arms; and William son of Richard Bulkelegh and William de Tranemol as archers. The last named joined Sir Robert's company. Upon his arrival in the Principality Sir Robert was appointed captain of the Prince's Household, a position of high honour normally granted to a person of noble birth; such a grant to a person of low birth must have caused friction in the Royal Household.

* * *

The Prince's army began by making *chevauchées* into the rebellious areas: they raided Armagnac, Périgord, Albret, Anjou, and Berry. Sir Hugh Calveley led 2,000 men against the Count of Armagnac, 'making disastrous war and doing great damage'. From Armagnac Sir Hugh went to join the Earl of Pembroke in Anjou, and then on to Saumer, finally gaining great acclaim for taking Pont de Cé on the

River Loire late in 1369. After a stay of five days at Angoulême, Sir Robert was sent into enemy territory with 600 men-at-arms and 500 mounted archers and 500 foot soldiers (probably both archers and spearmen). From Angoulême he marched to Agen where he remained a further five days. Whilst at Agen he received intelligence that Sir Perducas d'Albret, a Gascon nobleman, had sided with the French and immediately sent a herald to talk with his old comrade, for they had been fellow commanders in Spain. Sir Robert's plea was successful and his old comrade agreed to change sides.

From Agen Sir Robert joined up with Sir John Chandos in besieging the Priory of Duravel. The siege lasted five weeks but due to severe weather it had to be abandoned. From the priory the two companies marched to Domme, an important town in Quercy. Despite a siege there lasting fifteen days and many skirmishes, the two men achieved nothing and they therefore sought the Prince's permission to withdraw. On raising the siege Sir Robert went on to take the towns and castles of Figeac, Gramat, Fons, Rocamadour and Villefranche.

The routes taken by Sir Robert Knolles in 1369 - 70

The Prince of Wales recalled Sir John Chandos from Armagnac, and in consequence Sir Robert withdrew also, refusing to continue without his old comrade. The two returned to Angoulême in July 1369. Sir Robert then joined the forces of the Earls of Cambridge and Pembroke serving at the capture of La Roche-sur-Yon and then returned to base until the New Year. In January 1370, he accompanied the Prince to relieve the siege of Belleperche, and following their success received permission to return to his home at Derval in Brittany.

Sir Robert and many Englishmen were saddened at the news of the death of Sir John Chandos which occurred on 3 January 1370: he owned property in Cheshire and fought alongside many Cheshire men. On 31 December Sir John had ridden out of Poitiers with 300 men-at-arms to take the town of Saint-Savin-sur-Gartempe. After failing to take the place the valiant knight withdrew to Chauvigny for the night but most of his company continued through the night to reach safety at Poitiers. At dawn Sir John was informed that a French raiding party had ridden out of Saint Savin so he immediately armed himself and ordered his men to saddle up. He then chased the French, catching them at Lussac-Saint-Émillion where he dismounted and engaged them with his forty men.

> *... strong and bold knight and cool in his undertakings, advanced before him, surrounded by his men.... He himself was dressed in a large robe which fell to the ground, blazoned with his arms on white sarcenet, argent a pile gules, one on his breast the other on his back ; so that he appeared resolved on some adventurous undertaking and in this state, with sword in hand he advanced on foot towards the enemy. This morning there had been a hoar frost, which made the ground slippery; so that as he marched he entangled his legs with his robe, which was of the longest and made a stumble; during which time a squire called James de St. Martin, made a thrust at him with his lance, which hit him in the face, below the eye, between the nose and the forehead. Sir John did not see the aim of the stroke, for he had lost the eye on that side five years ago on the heaths of Bordeaux, at the chase of a stag. What added to this misfortune, Sir John had not put his visor down so that in stumbling, he bore upon the lance and helped it to enter into him...*

The small English force was beaten by the French, but shortly after the fight they were rescued by a force of Anglo-Gascons. Chandos, barely alive, was carried to the castle of Morthemer where two days later he died, his body then being interred at Lussac. Sir John Chandos, one of the original Knights of the Garter, High Constable of Aquitaine, Viscount of Saint-Sauveur, had been one of the Prince's closest friends. He had been one of his most able commanders and his loss was a serious blow to the English. 'Corteous and benign, amiable, liberal, preux, sage and true in all causes, nor was there ever a knight better beloved nor praised of every creature'.

A month earlier Sir James d'Audley of Helegh, the Seneschal of Poitou, had died of plague whilst garrisoned at Roche-sur-Yon so that by January 1370 not only had England lost two valiant heroes, she had also lost the provinces of Rougergue, Quercy, and much of Agenais region to the French.

Throughout the first half of the year the decline continued for du Guesclin was called from Spain to assist the French: he raided the Garonne valley and re-took many towns and castles from the English. Having arrived home in February 1370 Sir Robert was summoned to England and to Windsor to a council of war as intelligence had been received by King Edward to the effect that the French were contemplating an invasion of Wales; a large-scale invasion of France was therefore planned as a counter. Sir Robert Knolles was appointed to be the Commander in Chief of the coming invasion, an incredibly high position for one of 'inferior birth'. From the Feast of the Nativity of St John the Baptist, (24 June), Sir Robert's services were retained for two years. The deputy commanders were named as Sir Alan Buxhall, the Lord Grandison, and Sir John Bouchier.

On 18 July, the expeditionary force set sail for Normandy, embarking at Winchelsea and Rye, but contrary winds forced them to land at Calais. Four days later the army set off on its *chevauchée*; a force of 1,500 men-at-arms and 4,000 archers advanced into France. The host arrived at Thérouanne but found it too strong to attack, however, the next castle at Fiennes fell to them. Next the suburbs of Arras were burned to the ground; then on to Roye and through the province of Artois into Picardy; then on to Troyes and to Vermandois. The route used by Sir Robert was similar to that used by the King in the campaign to Reims in 1360; in fact, as in that year, Sir Robert also paraded his men before the walls of Paris to tempt the French to fight. The army provided for itself by means of plunder, and the French people fled before the invaders. Knolles wasted little time in laying siege to towns and castles; that was not his objective which was to lay as much of France waste, to take as many wealthy prisoners as possible and to keep the French occupied. At Noyon Sir Robert offered the French battle but were not satisfied. The city of Reims once again witnessed an English army at its gates, as did Paris on 22 September the army camped at Ablon-sur-Seine and two days later they drew up in battle order between Villejuif and Paris, but Charles V refused to do battle. Dejected, Sir Robert moved on to Saint Gervais-de-Sées and sacked the town following which he made for Brittany with the idea of settling around Derval for the winter.

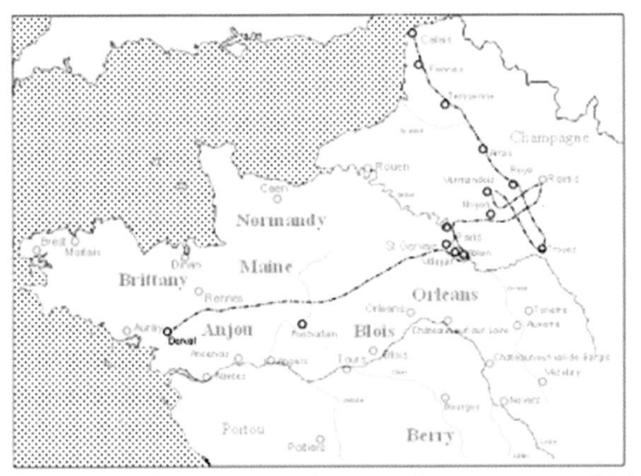

The route taken by Sir Robert Knolles in summer 1370

* * *

Throughout the campaign dissension grew in the army caused by the young nobles considering it beneath them to be led by Sir Robert. The ring leader of the 'anti-Knolles' faction was Sir John de Menstreworth who led a sizeable part of the army away from Sir Robert, including the Lord Grandison. Shortly after the desertion it was learned that du Guesclin was close by having been summoned from Aquitaine to deal with the invaders. Sir Robert decided to give battle and sent word for Sir Hugh Calveley and Sir Alan Buxhall who were operating in the Loire valley. He also sent for Grandison who returned to Sir Robert who, unfortunately, along with Buxhall, was ambushed by du Guesclin at Pont Vallain on 4 December. Sir Hugh, however, managed to avoid the ambush and met his kinsman travelling up from Saint Maurice-sur-Loire.

With the loss of Buxhall and Grandison Sir Robert then decided not to battle with his arch-enemy and instead continued his withdrawal back to Derval. Du Guesclin pursued Menstreworth's army and eventually overtook and defeated them in a skirmish in which nearly all were killed. Menstreworth himself managed to escape the melée and made for England where he claimed Sir Robert Knolles was the cause of the English army's defeat and that he was a traitor and deserter. On accepting the indictments against Sir Robert the court cancelled all his privileges and rights. John Stanley of Hooton, a squire in Knolles' company, was sent to Westminster to defend his master's reputation. Unexpectedly, Sir Alan Buxhall, having escaped from the encounter on the Loire, arrived at Westminster and added weight to Sir Robert's defence. The two advocates accepted that the campaign had ended in disaster, but that it was due not to Knolly's cowardice as was claimed, but to mutiny inspired by Menstreworth and that pride and disobedience by the lieutenants were the cause of the mutiny. Sir Robert was cleared and Menstreworth fled the country, and was himself branded a traitor.

Although Robert's campaign achieved little in recapturing towns and castles, it had taken the pressure off Aquitaine. Due to his overall failure Sir Robert was censured and had to buy back Royal favour, consequently a sum of 10,000 marks (£6,666) was sent to the King with Lord Latimer who subsequently embezzled most of the money and was later charged with the offence, but Knolles did manage to win back favour. In 1371, he was appointed Governor of Calais by John of Gaunt and in that capacity he attempted to retake the province of Ponthieu. On 22 June 1372, a large fleet left England under the command of John Hastings, Earl of Pembroke, to safeguard Aquitaine. Sir Robert accompanied the army which never reached its destination, for it was defeated by a large Castilian fleet, off La Rochelle. Although the Earl of Pembroke was captured, Sir Robert managed to escape and to return home.

* * *

During the Summer of 1373, Knolles was active in Brittany with Lord Neville and the Duke of Brittany, Jean de Montfort. When the province was again threatened by du Guesclin, Neville left for England to request aid leaving Sir Robert as Governor. Having been left an arduous task the newly appointed Governor brought his genius to bear. He strengthened various garrisons, including Derval, and placed a strong garrison at Brest leaving his home under the command of his cousin Sir Hugh Browe. He was born in the Malpas areas of Cheshire and, according to Froissart and heraldic sources, bore the same arms as Sir Robert which would certainly suggest a close family link.

The French, led by the Constable of France, an appointment du Guesclin had received in 1367, attacked Brest and laid siege to it. Du Guesclin then moved off to Derval, leaving Oliver de Clisson to keep the siege. On being threatened by a superior force, Browe decided to negotiate a truce to last for four months and that should the town not be relieved by then he would surrender. Louis Duke of Anjou, one of Guesclin's lieutenants, agreed to the terms on condition that no one should enter or leave the castle and that hostages be exchanged. Sir Robert on hearing of the plight of his home then negotiated a similar truce at Brest to last for forty days and on 9 July that siege was lifted. Sir Robert knew that a fleet under the command of the Earl of Salisbury was at sea nearby and a message to them brought the fleet with its large army near to Brest as insurance. With Brest temporarily safe Sir Robert set off for Derval.

On reaching the castle he manged to enter secretly with a number of men-at-arms. Once inside he sent word to the besiegers that the negotiations entered into by Browe were void and that he had no intention of giving the town and castle up to his enemy. Anjou and du Guesclin demanded an explanation from Knolles and were told that Browe had been given no authority to make such agreements and that had he known of the arrangements he, as captain of the castle, would not have consented. In retaliation the French had the hostages executed under the walls of the castle. In retaliation Sir Robert then had a scaffold built on the walls and had his prisoners, three knights and an esquire, executed and their bodies flung into the ditch below. The garrison then sallied out and soundly beat the dejected Frenchmen.

The next few years saw a rapid decline in the English rule in France. By the beginning of 1374, she possessed only the area around Calais and a thin coastal strip between Bordeaux and Bayonne. England's King was on the decline too, through old age, as was his son and heir, the Prince of Wales, who through ill health was slowly dying. In August 1373, John Duke of Lancaster, set out from Calais on a *chevauchée* in an attempt to bring the French to a decisive battle and to reclaim what had been lost. On 4 August an army of 15,000 left Calais, intending to march through eastern France and then cut across to Bordeaux. Although the army completed the journey they failed to bring the French to battle. Many skirmishes took place and in one of them, fought on 20 September, Sir Walter Hewitt was slain; rushing into a fray without his helmet he was pierced in the neck with a spear. Both Sir Hugh Calveley and Sir Robert Knolles were on the campaign and in one skirmish Sir Hugh lost eight of his men, and in another Sir Robert took the town of Niort, near Bordeaux. Both men returned to England in the late summer of 1374. Among the soldiers on the expedition were William le Barbour de Wyche Malbank (Nantwich) John le Parker of Copenhale, and Richard de Sydyngton.

On 8 June 1376 Edward, Prince of Wales, Earl of Chester, died. With the death of this beloved Englishman, the Black Prince, the 'Flower of English Chivalry', England's hopes of retaining her French dominions died. A truce between the two countries was arranged and, on 28 November, Sir Robert Knolles was appointed one of the conservators of the truce. At about the same time Sir Hugh was appointed Governor of the Channel Isles, a position of much importance which he continued to hold until 1388. The men of Cheshire had served their Prince and Earl well and in doing so they had served England too. The people of the county grew proud of their record in France; later generations remembered and recorded the events of their ancestors. Thomas Maisterson of Nantwich was remembered in the writings of his descendant Laurence who in 1611 wrote:

> *...went into Spain with Edward the Black Prince in that honourable Jorney wich he made for the restoringe of Peter King of Castill unto his Kingdome. He fought in the vanguard with Jo: of Gaunt duke of Lancaster aginst the French where Sir Bertram du Gleaqin constable of France, and the marshall Dandrehem were, which part of the army was in the cruelst fight, not with standinge, that Henry the Bastord, that usurped, restored and stayed his men thrise that day when they were at poynt to fly; for the great valour of the sayd Tho: shewed that day, upon there return to Burdeaux, the duke of Lancaster did wyn the said Thomas to his service, and by an indenture interchangeobly did bind him to serve in the wans upon honourable termes and honourable conditions and to pay him yerly the sum of x l. p. ann. out of his receipts of his honour of*

Holton, as by sayd Indenture may appeare. Upon their returne from Spaine he made his account with the Constable of Burdeaux and it was found that the Prince was behind with him for pay for himselph, his men-at-arms and archers the some of 2738 fortz of Gwyan gold which sayd money he could never be payd, although the hence appoynted his recevors in Cheshire, John Sonde and Jo: Allen, to make payment thereof to him...."

As late as 1387 Cheshire men were still receiving rewards for service to the Black Prince for in July of that year, the following were granted the franchise of the town of Middlewich in compensation for their services in France, Aquitaine and Spain: Robert Brotherson, Richard Gandy, William Wyng, Hugh de Legh, Robert de Newhall, Henry Cotton, and John de Crosslegh, all of Middlewich. Cheshire men-at-arms and archers had seen service in much of France; at Caen, Crecy and Calais; at Poitiers, in Brittany and other provinces. Not only did they serve, their contribution was a major part in the battles and campaigns, their skill at archery surpassing all others.

Many Cheshire people served the Earl of Chester in a non military capacity, for example: John de Legh as the 'yeoman of the buttery' to the Prince, and 'purveyor of his household'; John Hale was the Prince's clerk and keeper of his Privy Seal; Robert de Legh was bailiff of the Prince's manor of Macclesfield; and Richard Mascy was bailiff of the Prince's advowries in Cheshire. On 21 June, old King Edward died, but the men of Cheshire were to continue their military careers by serving his grandson, Richard II. The majority of Cheshire men were devoted to the son of the Black Prince and on them the young King relied heavily in times of trouble; but trouble of a domestic kind rather than external.

* * *

References for Chapter Seven

Much has been taken from *Froissart's Chronicles*, and *Rymer's Foedera*. Preparations for Knolles expedition will be found in Brantingham's *Issue Rolls*. *The Black Prince's Register* has again been consulted. The story of the death of Sir John Chandos has come from Froissart and an account in the *Dictionary of Chivalry* by Grant Uden. The account of the career of Thomas Maisterson is from Hall's *History of Nantwich*. J. Sumption, *Divided Houses: The Hundred Years War, Volume 3*(2002) the third of the excellent series on the Hundred Years Wars has been consulted.

* * *

POOLE
STARKEY
STANLEY
VERNON

8. CALVELEY, CRADDOCK AND KNOLLES

On 16 July, Richard of Bordeaux, son of Edward of Woodstock, Prince of Wales, was crowned King Richard II. The eleven-year old boy inherited little of his grandfather's French lands for they had been reduced to an area around Calais, a coastal strip around Bordeaux, and a few harbours in Brittany; what possessions England held were continually threatened by Charles V who was even contemplating an invasion of England.

Many Cheshire men continued to serve in France in the early years of Richard's reign in an effort to hold on. In 1377 the following men received letters of protection, all dated 15 September: Thomas son of William de Carynyngton, William de Carynyngton, Thomas Carynyngton and John de Leycestre, all of whom accompanied the King's uncle, Thomas, Earl of Buckingham, the Constable of England. On 15 May letters were issued to a number of men who were to accompany John of Gaunt, Duke of Lancaster, including Robert de Pilkyngton, esquire, then steward of the barony of Halton. In 1378 eight men went to Calais: Peter son of William, son of Phillip Chirchemunshull, William de Carynton and Thomas his son, William de Hoton, John de Pule, Thomas del Hogh, and William le Harper - apart from the first named who went with Sir Hugh Calveley, all the others accompanied Sir William Trussel of Warmingham. In April, Walter de Cockesaye, a knight from Salop who had inherited the Cheshire lands of the Saint Pierre family, went abroad with Thomas, Earl of Warwick. In June a Nicholas de Longeford went abroad with Hugh, Earl of Stafford.

In 1377 the French attacked the castle of Outwick, near Calais. The captain of the castle was a Cheshire knight, Sir William Weston, who frightened by the French use of cannon surrendered his charge and fled to the safety of Calais. The deputy keeper of Calais, Sir Hugh Calveley, hearing of the matter had Weston arrested and sent to London for trial, and then set off for the castle and within a day had recaptured it taking a number of prisoners and much booty.

Towards the end of the year a French fleet active in the English Channel raided a number of merchant ships carrying provisions to Calais; in one such raid a whole English fleet was lost. Sir Hugh furious at the losses in the Channel began to inflict punishment on the people who lived near to Calais. As the French pirates were using the port of Boulogne as a base he set off with a small fleet. Sailing close to the coast he came upon the port and managed to seize twenty-six vessels and set them on fire; he then sacked the town and returned to Calais again with many prisoners and much booty.

In December 1377 Sir Robert de Salle, governor of the castle of Marke, left for England leaving his charge to a number of English archers and a group of mercenaries from Picardy. During the captain's absence the English arranged an archery practice outside the walls of the castle and whilst the contest was under way the mercenaries allowed a French raiding party into the castle. On realising they had been tricked the archers sent word to Sir Hugh who immediately set off from Calais. Within twenty-four hours the castle was once more in English hands; all the mercenaries were executed. In the Spring of 1378 Sir Hugh had to deal with another incident of treachery. The Sire de Guienny, captain of Adres, surrendered his charge to the French and Sir Hugh had him taken into custody and sent to London for trial. Later in the same year he visited a grand fair which was being held at the town of Étaples, on the coast south of Boulogne. On arrival Sir Hugh wrecked the fair and sacked the town, taking a large quantity of provisions back to Calais.

Whilst Sir Hugh remained active around Calais Sir Robert was busy in Brittany. In 1377 he commanded a number of ships which set off with every intention of capturing a Castilian fleet of pirates at anchor off Sluys, however, bad weather forced him back to Brittany. In 1378 he defeated a French force just outside Brest and then in April of the same year he journeyed to England to join the Earl of Arundel in attacking the French at Harfleur. In 1379 the port of St. Malo, in northern Brittany, was besieged by John, Duke of Lancaster and on this occasion his lieutenant was Sir Robert Knolles. Following the siege Sir Robert and his cousin, Sir Hugh Browe, plundered the neighbouring countryside and later that year accompanied John de Montfort to London before returning with him to Vannes.

During this same year Sir Hugh was commissioned as one of two Admirals of the Fleet; the other being Sir Thomas Percy. Putting to sea to celebrate his appointment he took several French merchant ships and one Castillian galleon and sent them to Bristol. Whilst the siege of St. Malo was in progress Sir Hugh, 'our admiral', was sent to the port with the Duke of Britanny: their fleet consisted of a number of merchant ships. They landed at a haven near to the port and once they had entered this they were attacked by the French. Sir Hugh ordered his armed ships to turn about, '... *through the manfull prowess of Sir Hugh, the galleys were repelled, for, according to his wonted valliancie, he would not return till he saw all others in safetie.....*'. In 1379 an incident occurred which indicates the respect and fear the Frenchmen had for Sir Hugh. Sir Geoffrey de Cormel, a Breton knight, ambushed a party of English soldiers but then on learning that they were part of Sir Hugh's retinue he immediately released them. He did more than that - he sent them home with apologies to Sir Hugh and promises of castles, horses and provisions.

* * *

During that year a number of official letters of protection were issued to Cheshire people on behalf of their Earl. On 5 January 1379 John, son of Robert Bulkelegh of Eton, received letters on going to defend the castle of Cherbourg, in Normandy; on 17 February, William, son of William, son of Phillip de Churchemunshull received letters on going abroad with John d'Arundel, captain of Cherbourg; on 18 June, Thomas de Caryngton on going with Sir Hugh Calveley; and on 5 October, Sir Thomas Danyell on going with Sir John Devereaux.

Towards the end of the year an expedition was planned to Brittany to support Knolles and de Montfort. The planned expedition was to be led by Sir Hugh Calveley and Sir John d'Arundel, Earl of Arundel, but due to severe storms it failed and twenty vessels and a thousand men were lost in the Atlantic, including the Earl. It was thought that Sir Hugh too was lost and the royal court mourned his loss for several days. Fortunately Sir Hugh who had manged to cling to wreckage was dashed against the Irish coast and after a few weeks had managed to return to London. The wreck was put down to 'God's revenge' upon Arundel who on a previous expedition to France had sacked a nunnery.

At the end of July 1380 Thomas of Woodstock, Earl of Buckingham, mustered troops for a large-scale invasion of Brittany to aid its Duke. Finance for the expedition was a problem as the royal coffers were empty and consequently Sir Hugh, recently appointed Captain of Brest, was kept waiting with 1,000 men outside London. Eventually the Mayor of London raised sufficient funds to pay the troops and they set off for France. Sir Hugh led the vanguard of the army which landed at Calais and then travelled through Artois, Picardy, Vermandois and Champagne, eventually reaching the valley of the river Loire which they then followed into Brittany. During the campaign it was learnt that the town of Péronne had been occupied by the Seneschal of Hainault so Sir Hugh went to the town with nine men. Seeing Sir Hugh and thinking him stupid to approach the gates with so few the Seneschal sallied out to take him. Sir Hugh immediately turned and led the French into an ambush: the majority of the French were captured by Sir Hugh's company but the Seneschal escaped - Péronne was again garrisoned by the English. During the same year Sir Hugh and his men figured in many skirmishes: for example he chased a French party under the Lord Hargest to Plancy and he appeared at the siege of Nantes.

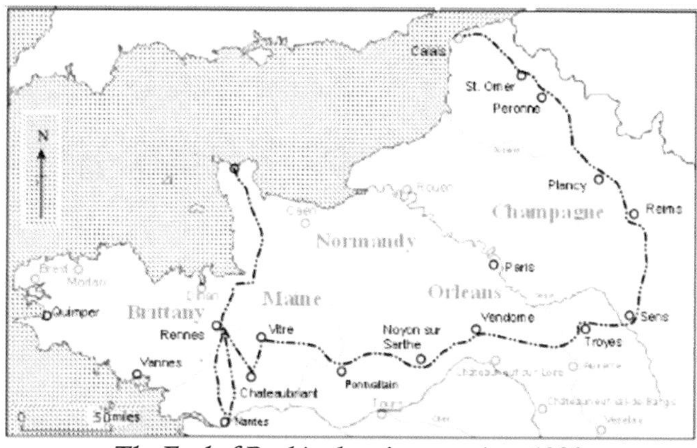

The Earl of Buckingham's campaign, 1380.

Sir Robert also went on the expedition into Brittany and when near Vendôme his retinue was involved in a skirmish with a company of French led by the Sire de Mauvoisin whom they defeated and Sir Robert took the leader prisoner. Sir Robert took part in the siege at Rennes where Buckingham eventually set his headquarters. At the end of November he was at the siege of Nantes and was stationed at St. Nicholas' Gate with Sir Thomas Percy. Sir Robert's valour in an incident at the gate on 12 November is said to have saved the English army from defeat. By the end of 1380 Montfort's support for England was beginning to waver. On one occasion Sir Robert was sent by Buckingham to negotiate with Montfort in an effort to retain his support which was ultimately lost and the siege werewas called off. On 2 January 1381, Buckingham retired to Vannes, and Sir Robert and Sir Hugh left for Quimper before embarking for England where they arrived in April.

Of other Cheshire men on the campaigns in France we find Sir Hugh Browe with letters of protection dated 2 July 1380 about to depart with Buckingham and Knolles; Sir John de Pulle on going with Sir Hugh Calveley on the same date; Sir John Danyell on going with Knolles; and Sir Richard Mascy on going with William, Lord Latimer. During 1381 and 1382 a few men went over to France from Cheshire: Nicholas Grimesdyche received letters of protection in April 1381; on 28 May 1382 Sir John Mascy of Potington went to Cherbourg with the warden of the castle there, Sir William Windsor, and on 5 November 1382 Robert de Mascy went to Calais with John Devereaux.

* * *

In 1383 Sir Hugh Calveley was appointed to lead a 'crusade' in support of Pope Urban against the supporters of the 'anti-pope' Clement. This so called crusade was financed by the Church at the request of the warlike Bishop of Norwich.

The expeditionary force landed at Calais on 23 April where they waited for support from the Earl Marshal, Sir William Beauchamp. Whilst waiting Sir Hugh went to visit an old colleague in Calais, Sir John Drayton, and during his absence plans were made by senior figures in the army to defend Flanders against the French which was contrary to the oath they had all made prior to leaving England. On hearing of the new plan Sir Hugh would have none of it, but was eventually persuaded otherwise and therefore reluctantly went along with the majority.

The 'crusade' took the towns of Dunkirk and Gravelines and laid siege to Ypres and what successes the expeditionary force had were largely due to sir Hugh's experience, but at Bergues, a French army lay in wait. The French, led by their King, were so strong that battle was pointless so the 'crusaders' withdrew. The expedition had been a complete disaster and on return to England many of the knights were imprisoned for breaking their oaths and the Bishop was censured, but Sir Hugh, because of his initial reluctance, was pardoned.

Robert Cotton of Cotton, a Cheshire squire, served in the 'crusade' under Sir Thomas Carrington, with a man-at-arms and three archers. At Ypres Richard Craddock of Nantwich was taken prisoner; he was released after a year when his father David Cradock, then the Mayor of Bordeaux, the Archbishop of Bordeaux, and the Abbot of St. Croix in Bordeaux, had paid his ransom.

David Craddock, son of Nicholas Craddock, was a member of a family who held lands in Weston, near Crewe; the family also held lands in Alvaston and Nantwich. David was born in 1335 and was educated in law at London. He became attorney to his uncle, the Bishop of Waterford, in 1356. In 1374 he received a grant of £40 a year from the Prince of Wales which was to be paid out of the Welsh Exchequer, then, on 6 July, he was appointed fiscal head of North Wales, as 'Chamberlain and Receiver of Dues' and a further £1 a year. On 8 June 1376 he 'delivered' to Joan, the Prince's widow, her dower of rents, issues and properties, which the Prince had held in Wales. In November he delivered the remainder of the Prince's estate, including the Earldom of Chester, to Richard of Bordeaux, the Prince's son. On 3 November, David Craddock was appointed Justice of North Wales and in the same month he was also made Justice of South Wales - two extremely important posts. So far as the administration of Wales was concerned, in both a judicial and fiscal capacity, he was the most important personage next to the Prince himself. In 1380 he was created custodian of Beaumaris Castle in Anglesey with a further annuity of £40; he was already custodian of the castle at Conway and Mayor of its town.

The years 1379 to 1381 saw troubled times in Wales, and Sir David, as he was by then, was instrumental in keeping matters under control but his methods were harsh and in some instances too harsh so that many complaints were made about him to Westminster. In 1382 Sir David lost his positions in Wales and was sent to Bordeaux as the town's mayor and was granted letters of protection on 12 June that year. In August he journeyed to meet Carlos of Navarre and to treat with him on behalf of King Richard. In 1384 he retired from royal service to settle back home in Nantwich. Although a contemporary of Sir Hugh and Sir Robert he was not primarily a soldier but a Cheshire man who served both Edward Prince of Wales and Richard II in a civil capacity and held high office. Richard Craddock, David's son and heir, was born in 1362 and when aged nineteen went on the 'crusade' as we have heard. On 26 August 1389 Richard went to defend the castle of Fronsac, in the Girande valley, in south-west France. In the following year he, with Sir William d'Elingham, went to Aquitaine upon the King's command according to orders issued to the 'keeper of the passage of the port of Dover' with a commission for the '*...reformation of certain misprisons committed* *by the King's vassals there contrary to the present truce between the King and his adversary of France and to suffer them to pass thither with eight man-at-arms, twenty archers and other yeomen and servants to the number of fifty mounted men, taking their bows and arrows, horses money goods and harness whatsoever ...*'. During 1391, 1392, and 1393, Sir Richard Craddock remained in south-west France as a soldier and legal administrator.

* * *

After the campaign of 1380 service in France was limited to garrison duties at castles still held by the English for there were no major campaigns. In 1388, when England and France were formally at peace, English knights and esquires travelled to France to engage in various feats of arms in tournaments - the chief sport of the age of chivalry for which men journeyed great distances to take part. French, English, Spanish, Germans and others would travel throughout Europe to display their valour and skill with the lance or sword. The meetings were occasions for great pageantry: coloured tents (pavillions) were erected around the field, arms were displayed on tunics, shields, banners, pennons, and horse trappings. Fairs were held with market stalls, sideshows and entertainers. In many ways these were the equivalent of modern events such as international sporting events. The tournament was an occasion when a poor landless squire could prove himself a valiant combatant, and be recognised by military commanders.

One such event was held at St. Inglevert in 1388. It was arranged by a number of French knights who challenged all comers to a feat of arms. The French knights were Sir Reginald de Roye, Sir Bouciquant and Sir John II de Sempy. Outside their tents these three knights exhibited their shields: they displayed two shields, one with their arms of war, the other with their arms of peace. A challenger would be expected to touch either of the shields depending upon the choice of weapons and the type of event then the match would be fought with either blunted weapons to prevent serious hurt 'armes a plaisance', or with real weapons of war, 'a l'outrance'. In the four days over which the jousts were run, more than forty challengers took up arms in one hundred and thirty-six courses. A large number of Englishmen were attracted to the tournament, held near Calais, eager to prove themselves against the French. Three Cheshire men took part: John Savage, whose descendants armoured effigies lie in Macclesfield church', Thomas Mascy and William Mascy. Bernard

Stapleton may also have been from Cheshire. Savage fought on Tuesday 22 May and his encounter went as follows:

> *...an English squire, a good tilter, called John Savage, squire of honour and of the body to the Earl of Huntingdon, sent to touch the shield of sir Reginald de Roye. The knight answered, he was ready and willing to satisfy him. When he had mounted his horse, and had his helmet buckled and lance given to him, they set off full gallop, and gave such blows, on the targets, that had the spears not broken, one or both must have fallen to the ground. This course was handsome and dangerous; but the knights received no hurt, though the points of the lances passed through the targets, and slipped off their side-armour. The spears were broken about a foot from the shaft, the points remaining in the shields; and they gallantly bore the shafts before them, as they finished their career. The spectators thought they must have been seriously wounded; and the French and English hastened each to their companion, whom, to their joy, they found unhurt. They were told they had done enough for that day but John Savage was not satisfied, and said he had not crossed the sea for only one tilt with a lance. This was reported to sir Reginald, who replied, 'He is in the right; and it is but just that he should be gratified, either by me or by one of my companions'. When they had rested themselves a while, and received new lances, they began their second course, each aiming well at the other; but they failed, from the swerving of their horses, to their great vexation, and returned to their posts. Their lances, which had been accidentally dropped, were given to them, and they set off on their third course. This time they hit on the vizors of their helmets; and, by the force and crossing of their lances, both were unhelmed as they passed. The tilt was much applauded for its correctness and vigour. When they were returned to their posts, the English told John Savage, that he had very honourably performed, and that it was now time for him to make way for others to tilt as well as himself. He complied with this, and, laying aside his lance and target, dismounted, and rode on a hackney to witness the performances of others.*

Thomas Mascy had ridden earlier on the same day, but had not been so successful:

> *... Then a young knight of England, richly armed, named Thomas Mascy; he touched the shield of war, of Sir Bouciquant. He was immediately answered. The first course they crossed on*

the helms. The second course they met and Thomas broke his spear into truncheons, and Bouciquant struck him so sore, that he bore him to the earth over his horses back. Thomas' company took him and he jousted no more...

William Mascy ran a course with Bouciquant in which both were unhelmed:

...Another English knight, called sir William Masquelee, was ready to enter the lists, and to engage with whoever pleased; for he had crossed the sea with the Earl of Huntingdon in this view. He sent to touch the war-target of sir Boucicaut, who had his buckler fastened, and instantly advanced to meet his adversary. They both at the same moment spurred their horses, which were fresh and eager to begin the course; for the very instant they felt the points, they bounded forward. The two knights took good aim, and mutually gave such strokes on their helmets that fire sparkled from them; and, though the points of the lances slipped off, the tilt was much praised by all present. They continued their career to their different stations, but did not make any long stay before they again spurred their horses and couched their spears, for they did not drop them, and met with such violence, that their lances must have pierced the bucklers, if the horses had not swerved. They finished their course, throwing down their lances, and completed their career like good tilters, in excellent array to their posts. Having received their spears, they set off as fast as their horses could carry them, and, on their meeting, hit the vizors of the helmets severely. The tilt was loudly applauded, for they were both unhelmed, and bare-headed all but the scull-caps: they finished their career, and then returned to their friends, for they had excellently performed.

Stapleton went against Saimy:

...Bernard Stapleton, an English squire, sent to strike the lord de Saimpy's shield, who was not dismounted from his last tilt. They met, and hit each other on the helmets so forcibly as to make the sparks fly from them; but they passed on without hurt and returned to their posts. Still grasping their spears, they couched them, and at this second course struck very severe blows on their targets, but kept their seats well, without falling or staggering, to the end of their career. The third lance struck the helmets, and

both were unhelmed. The English squire returned from the lists, as his friends told him he had acquitted himself with honour.

* * *

References for Chapter Eight

The Chronicles of John Froissart; *The History of Nantwich* by James Hall; *The History of Cheshire*by G. Ormerod. *The Black Prince's Register*, Parts l & lll; J. Sumption, *Divided Houses: The Hundred Years War, Volume 3* (2002) the third of the excellent series on the Hundred Years Wars has been consulted.

* * *

SAVAGE

MASCY of PODDINGTON

CARRINGTON

CRADOCK

COTTON

LEYCESTER

9. THE LIVERY OF THE STAG

Richard II was born at Bordeaux on 6 January 1367, the son of Edward, Prince of Wales, and Joan of Kent. In the summer of his tenth year he was crowned King. He was not a strong youth; he had a pale complexion and fair hair, his speech had a slight defect, but he was tall and good looking. He grew up in his mother's company and she and her friends doted upon him, spoiling and flattering him. In growing up amongst a tight-knit circle of friends and relations who instilled into him the divine right of kingship he lacked any confidence and qualities of firmness. Without his close friends he felt insecure. The unfortunate upbringing of the impressionable boy produced a tyrannical sovereign and brought about his eventual downfall. A tyrant needs a completely loyal and experienced body of men to do his bidding without question - Richard found such a body of men in Cheshire, as we shall learn.

During his minority Richard's uncles struggled for control of the country. John, D,, Duke of York, and Thomas, Duke of Gloucester, all sought to influence the young King. A council was created representing all parties to advise on the ruling of the country. Both Lancaster and Gloucester sought to control the country's military affairs but Parliament appointed two London merchants as 'treasureres of war': William Wallworth and John Philpot who were to control the use of monies from taxation for military matters.

Money was desperately needed to protect the south coast from regular attacks by the French and to finance the invasions of 1379 and 1380. In 1380 a Poll Tax was levied on the whole population. Taxes had been rising constantly since the start of the reign and the Government of the day was unpopular but tis new tax became the 'straw that broke the camel's back' and the ordinary people of England rebelled. The peasantry became lawless, and attacked the rich and the tax officials. The time was ripe for the agitators of the day. Wycliffe preached against the power and wealth of the Church; Wat Tyler of Kent stirred the people of south-east England into rebellion; the people of Essex, led by Jack Straw, were in revolt too.

On 13 June 1381 two large bands of peasants moved towards London. In the city the gates were opened to them by sympathisers. The Archbishop of Canterbury was murdered, Lancaster's palace at Savoy was burned to the ground, and the King and his Court were besieged in the Tower of London. For two days the pillage of the

City continued unhindered. Sir Robert Knolles in his house close to that of Lancaster's at the Savoy, 'guarded his treasure with over six-score fighting men all in readiness .... would have sallied out at once had the word been given'. Sir Robert was sent for to advise the young King on what to do; he urged diplomacy and consequently negotiations with the rebels commenced. The King went out to meet the rebels at Mile End in East London and there he conceded to certain demands and many of the insurgents left.

On Saturday 15 June King Richard, accompanied by Sir Robert Knolles and others went to Smithfield to meet the remaining rebels. Sir Robert, with a force of men-at-arms, was one of the first to arrive. With Sir Perducas d'Albret and the nine Aldermen, each with their own forces, there were about 600 men in the royal party. On reaching Smithfield the King dubbed three new knights: William Wallworth, Mayor of London, John Standish and Nicholas Brembre. King Richard then asked Knolles if the rebels should be killed but was told that should not as many were there against their wills. The King then ordered the people to disperse but Tyler approached the King and made such outrageous demands that Sir Robert flew into a rage and, despite his initial advice to the king, asked permission to attack. Permission was refused and the King continued to speak to the majority, who, hearing his promises, began to move away. Tyler then became even more aggressive and made threats to the King's party whereupon Wallworth pulled Tyler from his horse and Standish plunged his sword into his stomach.

Later, Sir Robert, the Mayor of London and others were ordered to round up any other malefactors and were given authority to behead and mutilate those caught. On 23 June the freedom of the City of London was conferred upon Sir Robert for his part in putting the rebellion down. He was also granted the rare privilege of building, between two of his properties, a 'hautepas' (a hallway on pillars extending over a street). Later in the same year he was granted the manor of St. Pancras, London. The 'Peasants Revolt' continued for a few more years and Sir Robert was engaged in tracking down the various pockets of rebellion.

* * *

As Richard grew into manhood he continually quarrelled with his uncles, especially Gaunt, as to the running of the country. The King handed out gifts to his loyal friends on such a scale that his uncles became envious. One of Richard's closest friends was Robert de Vere, Earl of oxford, on whom he heaped many rewards; he was granted large estates and the title Earl of Suffolk in 1385; later in the same year he was elevated to be England's first Marquis, and in 1386 he was granted the title Duke of Ireland. The King relied on his powerful Court officials to support him against his uncles and their 'political parties'. The court party was comprised of his tutor, Sir Simon Burley, his controller of the wardrobe, Sir Baldwin Raddington, and Sir Michael de la Pole, his guardian and chancellor. With the growth of the various parties rumours became rife: it was said that Gaunt was plotting against the King; that the King was plotting to do away with Gaunt; that a faction led by the Earl of Arundel had rebuked the king for bad governance, and so on.

Whilst these rumours spread throughout England France decided upon an invasion of England with her ally Scotland. The French plan was slow to start and England took the defensive by initiating a campaign against Scotland. The retinues of the great magnates were to be at Newcastle on Tyne by 14 July 1385. The size of the army assembled amounted to 4,600 men-at-arms and 9,100 archers. The King, Lancaster, Buckingham and the Earl of Northumberland were the leaders of largest retinues: Lancaster led 1,000 men-at-arms and 3,000 archers. Cheshire as usual provided a large number of men. Several months earlier Cheshire men had gone to the northern marches in defence of England. Four men from one family had letters of protection on going to Berwick on Tweed with Henry Percy, Earl of Northumberland, on 27 November 1384: Peter, Thomas and Geoffrey, sons of Thomas Starkey of Stretton, and Roger son of Geoffrey Starkey of Comberbach. Of the letters of protection issued in the summer we also find those of Robert Daniel of Ridley, who accompanied John Deveros; Vivian Foxwist and Sir Ralph de Vernon of Shipbrook, who accompanied Hugh de Segrave, Treasurer of England; Richard le Bailiff de Spurstow in the 'King's service'; and John, son of William de Hulgeave.

The campaign was not spectacular; the army sacked the abbeys of Melrose, Newbattle and Holyrood, and they burned the City of Edinburgh. Due to arguments as to strategy between the King and Lancaster, the invasion force withdrew. The costly event had done nothing except, perhaps, reduce the threat of a French-Scottish invasion.

During the campaign Sir Richard Scrope, baron of Bolton, met Sir Robert Grosvenor of Eaton, Cheshire. The two knights realised that they bore the same coat of arms, '*Azure, a bend, Or*' (a blue shield with a broad, diagonal gold band). This 'Age of Chivalry' was very much the age of heraldry and the bearing of arms and badges was a highly personalised matter. Scrope, who was Chancellor of England and Steward of the King's Household and had been once Treasurer of England, had experienced something similar previously. In I380 on returning from overseas he had met a Cornishman, named Carminow, displaying the same arms. A committee of knights arbitrated on the matter as each man claimed ancient usage. Scrope stated his family had used the arms since the times of the Normans and Carminow claimed that his family had been granted the arms by King Arthur! The committee decided that Cornwall was a separate country with its own rights and customs and therefore they allowed each family to continue to use the same arms. But the Scrope/Grosvenor case had a different outcome.

In August 1385, Sir Richard took his dispute with Grosvenor to the Court of Chivalry, the military court of the Constable of England and the Earl Marshal. Thomas, Duke of Gloucester, Constable and President of the Court, ordered that witnesses be sought and interviewed. Accordingly depositions were to be taken so that he might decide upon the matter between Scrope and Grosvenor. For four years evidence was gathered with enquiries held at York, Leicester, Nottingham, Westminster, Plymouth, Tiverton, Chester and elsewhere. On 1 October 1386 and 6 May 1388 hearings were held at Nantwich when knights and esquires of the county of Cheshire gave evidence to say that the Grosvenor family had borne the arms for generations and that their arms were displayed in many churches and had been seen at many battles. Adam Bostock, John Holford and many others gave evidence in Nantwich Church. Sir Hugh Browe stated on oath that he was forty years old and in support of his evidence he outlined his military career. He stated that he had never been on any great expedition but had been on various garrison duties in France. He had accompanied the Earl of March to Brittany; had accompanied the Duke of Buckingham in 1380; had been at the Siege of St. Malo two years earlier; in 1387 he had been part of the Earl of Arundel's naval retinue and that for his services to that Earl had been granted lands at Trafford and Dunham, in Cheshire.

After all the evidence had been gathered, it was found that its quantity and value was equal to each side: neither had infringed upon the other and each had shown evidence of ancient usage.

However, Gloucester found in favour of Scrope for he was an important person in the kingdom and was known on the continent and therefore to alter his arms would cause confusion, therefore his arms were to remain as they had always been. The Court's decision with regard to Grosvenor and a retrospective decision on the earlier case of Carminow. The verdict was that the arms of Grosvenor and Carminow had to made different with the addition of small 'charges'. Grosvenor was to add a silver border and Carminow a silver square in the top left of the shield. Grosvenor was not satisfied and appealed to the King and on 27 May 1390 the case was reopened before Richard II. The King upheld the decision of the Court of Chivalry but added that the addition of a border was an insufficient difference for two non-related families; he therefore granted the family a completely new coat of arms, '*Azure, a garb, Or*' (a blue shield with a wheatsheaf), in honour of the family's ancient ties with the Norman Earls of Chester - the family have had those arms ever since.

* * *

On returning from Scotland King Richard supported his uncle John's claim to the throne of Castile; John of Gaunt had married Constance an heiress to the Castillian throne. King Richard helped to finance the expedition and gave it his blessing and as John held lands in Cheshire a number of Cheshire men went with him. Sir Robert Knolles, Sir Thomas Fogg, Thomas Maisterson, and Robert de Pylkyngton, steward of Halton, all attended John as his lieges: others such as Richard Mascy, John Holford, Thomas Holford, William Chetwynd, and Sir John le Strange also served him. With the Duke in Castile King Richard felt easy and able to do his will.

In 1386 a threat of invasion was the reason for many Cheshire men going to the coast 'in defence of the realm'. For example, David Crowton of Nantwich, David de Eddersleg h, Robert le Grosvenor, John son of Henry Hickson de Pulford, Robert de Legh, and John le Typper de Halton. Once de Vere's had been made Duke of Ireland he set off to visit his duchy. The newly appointed Duke had Sir John Stanley of Hooton as his deputy, and many men followed de Vere and Stanley to Ireland. During 1386 and 1387 the following had letters of protection: Hugh d'Arderne, Robert de Bradbury, Reginald Downs, Thomas del Downes, Henry del Halle, Hugh son of Oliver de Mascy, and Thomas de Whalley of Wheelock, to name but a few.

Following Gaunt's departure for Castile, Gloucester and his faction decided to make their mark in governing the Kingdom. Gloucester's faction included the Earls of Arundel, Warwick and Nottingham. Having inherited little wealth as the youngest of Edward III's sons, Gloucester had to depend upon his ingenuity to gain power and fortune; he was unscrupulous and self seeking and was extremely jealous of his brother John's power: he had little time for his nephew, the King.

Once again England was threatened with invasion, so the King appealed to Parliament for help. The Commons refused their financial aid and refused to deal with the King's advisors, especially the Chancellor, de la Pole, and the Treasurer, Segrave. Parliament demanded their dismissal. Richard refused. A delegation led by Gloucester imposed themselves on Richard and ordered that Pole be dismissed. Richard surrendered and Pole was impeached, fined and imprisoned. Gloucester then appointed a commission to supervise the governing of the country and the King's Household.

Richard was humiliated by the decisions of Parliament and drew his friends closer to him. Without his seals of office Richard was powerless to fight back and was unable to levy forces about him to defend his rights as king against Gloucester. The Great Seal of England was not required in the County of Chester as the county had long been regarded as a separate state with its own rights, laws and customs; it was a County Palatine where the word of the Earl of Chester was law and Richard was its Earl. The same applied to Wales, of which he was Prince. Richard embarked on a tour of the midlands and the north in the spring and summer of 1387 and took with him de Vere, Burley and Raddington, the last being an experienced soldier and military purveyor. The tour became a recruitment drive with Richard collecting together a large personal army, the core of which was founded in Cheshire. It is at this time that the chroniclers of the time first refer to Richard's personal affinity to the county and his bodyguard of Cheshire men. By the end of the year de Vere had the command of Richard's army. There can be little doubt that Richard had had a bodyguard since the day he came to the throne; his father and grandfather had guards formed by Cheshire archers. Having learned of the Cheshire men's skills he set off to enlarge his bodyguard's numbers.

Whilst away Richard secretly contacted his judges in London and secured from them a ruling that the 'Commission' was illegal; thus armed, militarily and legally, Richard returned to London to assert his rights. De Vere was left in Cheshire to continue the recruitment. Gloucester hearing of the ruling and of Richard's advance appealed to Parliament and the officials of the City of London who over-ruled the judges' decision. Richard had been out-manoeuvred.

De Vere heard of the setback and set off from Cheshire with his new army: the Cheshire men were led by Thomas Molyneux, Constable of Chester Castle. But, Gloucester, assisted by Henry Bolinbroke, the eldest son to John of Gaunt, anticipated the move and set off to intercept de Vere. At Radcot Bridge, near Eynsham, on the river Thames, the two forces met. De Vere's total strength numbered 4,000; the Cheshire men following the banners of Molyneux, Sir Ralph Vemon, and Sir Ralph Ratcliffe. Gloucester's force was numbered similarly. On 20 December, in a fog, a brief flank attack on the Cheshire men put them to flight; de Vere managed to escape across the Thames to the south coast and then into exile in France. Molyneux was not so fortunate: he was captured and killed. It was a bitter blow to Richard and a triumph for Gloucester.

Worried, Richard was forced to imprison or banish his friends and advisors. At the Parliament in February 1388 the former method of impeachment by the House of Commons was abolished and a direct form of 'appealing' an accused by the Lords took its place. The 'Lords Appellant', Gloucester, the Earls of Derby, Arundel, Warwick, and Nottingham, accused Richard's ministers of various offences which resulted in Pole and de Vere being exiled.

* * *

After 1388 matters in England were relatively quiet and Richard gradually managed to build up a new circle of friends, one of whom, Thomas Mowbray, Earl of Nottingham, was made Justiciar of Chester and North Wales. In 1389 John of Gaunt returned to England and he produced a stabilising effect upon the government of the country. Richard and his uncle John began to respect one another and work together. In that same year, Richard declared himself of age and free to take on the responsibilities of kingship without restraint. He, with Lancaster as his Chief Councillor, ruled England. In 1392 the City of London was fined for its support of Gloucester and certain other individuals were punished for their support of him. For about six years Richard ruled without serious incident and was able to relax and pursue a life of luxury and extravagance.

In the Summer of 1394 his Queen, Anne, died and her death caused him much grief. When Richard's old enemy arrived late for her funeral Richard flew into a rage and struck the Earl of Arundel in the face. In an effort to forget his mourning Richard mounted an expedition to Ireland which was cost the exchequer 20,000 pounds a year. Ireland was in revolt against her English rulers and in October 1394 an expedition set sail, under the banner of King Edward the Confessor - a hero to the Irish. Many Cheshire men followed the 'Seigneur d'Ireland', for example, Roger son of William Jodrell of Yearsley, Robert de Legh, Richard de Wistaston, John son of William de Hulgreave, and Sir Robert de Whitney, Marshal of the King's Household. The expedition was a success, and Richard won the hearts of the Irish people. After eight months he returned leaving the Earl of March to continue the good work.

In July 1397 Richard suddenly took his revenge on his old enemies; he had the Earls of Warwick and Arundel along with the Duke of Gloucester arrested. At the Michaelmas Parliament of 1397 the Earls were 'appealed' by their own system and accordingly condemned. Arundel was sentenced to death and Warwick was sent into exile. The Duke of Gloucester was murdered in Calais before he was able to come to trial. Richard FitzAlan, the Earl of Arundel, was led to the block by a guard of Cheshire archers.

The Michaelmas Parliament of 1397 had been a show of strength by Richard. During the 'trial' the hall at Westminster was surrounded by Richard's bodyguard of Cheshire archers who numbered about 400, and when there appeared to be a commotion in the Hall, the archers drew their bows, fearing for the king's safety:

> *...thereupon the King's archers...... surrounded the parliament house which was set up to this end in the middle of the palace-yard, thought that some quarrel or strife had arisen in the house, and, bending their bows they drew their arrows to the ear to the great terror of all who were there, but the King quietened them...*

No doubt the time of the commotion coincided with Richard's statement that the laws of the land existed in his own breast. It is no wonder, in view of the pressure and threat they were under, that Parliament found the Earls guilty. The hall at Westminster was then a temporary structure without walls, so it was possible for the whole of the guard to surround the place and to threaten its occupants. What do we know of this bodyguard of Cheshire archers?

The men who formed the elite corps were described by contemporary chroniclers as 'arrogant insolent ruffians who were on far too intimate terms with the King'; 'malefactors from the county of Chester'; 'men who are naturally bestial and ready for any iniquity'; 'they treated the people with contempt and were guilty of theft violence and adultery, yet no redress was possible since the Chester men were favourites of the King'; 'they were raised from the low born and were insolent to their superiors, they considered themselves equal to nobles'. Low born was perhaps an apt description for many scions of the Cheshire knightly classes were attracted to the service by regular and high rates of pay and grants of offices and lands. The men of the guard wore the now commonplace green and white uniforms with on their shoulder Richard's badge - a white hart. They were often referred to as the archers of 'the livery of the stag' or of 'the white hart'.

The guard was split into 'watches' who guarded the King day and night, wherever he might be. Each watch comprised of a captain and about forty-five men. Originally there were six watches, but by Michaelmas 1398 there were seven. The captains were: Thomas de Beeston, Adam de Bostock, Richard de Cholmondeley, Ranulph de Davenport, Thomas de Holford, John de Legh de Booths. By the Michaelmas Parliament, Cholmondeley had been replaced by his son Thomas, and the extra captain, John Done of Utkinton had been appointed. These captains were known as the 'masters of the watches' and they continually accompanied the King and boasted of their intimacy with him.

In addition to the men of the bodyguard, 'who pleaded their case with pole axe and sword', the King recruited a large army. Men were recruited for life or 'during the King's pleasure'. Following the Michaelmas Parliament hundreds of Cheshire men took 'the livery of the Crown' in one form or another. From 1 July 1397 to 3 July 1398, a total of 377 men received grants of 6d a day, of whom all bar fifty of them were retained for life; in addition another 60 received wages of 4d, 3d or 2d a day and only two of whom were 'during pleasure'. In the same period 116 men received annuities of either 100s, ten marks, twenty marks, forty marks, £10, £11 13s 4d, £20 or £40. Of these only ten were granted 'during pleasure'.

The majority of men took service with the crown as archers, for example, John de Hulgreave, who, 'having heard that the King was desirous of being served by his lieges of Chester, and the said John being anxious to serve him prays to be admitted to his service', he was accordingly recruited and granted 6d a day. The grants to the archers are variously worded: ‘a grant of the livery of the Crown'; 'an appointment as a yeoman of the livery of the Crown', or, 'an appointment as an archer of the livery of the Crown'. In the margin of the rolls in which the appointments appear, some of the entries have the notation, 'sagittarius de Corona' (archer of the Crown), or simply 'archer'; 137 have such a notation. Are those with a marginal note those who were recruited to the actual bodyguard and those with simple grants of the livery being members of the army? One hundred and two men were appointed as 'yeoman'; thirty-eight were appointed as 'archers' and the remaining 227 were given simple 'grants of the livery'.

Amongst the men-at-arms, that is those who received annuities, there were twelve knights, seven esquires and fourteen armigers (ordinary men-at-arms who were not aspirants to knighthood as was the esquire). The captains of the watch were either esquires or armigers and in addition to the archers each watch had a number of men-at-arms, but the majority of them served in the main army.

Following his conviction Arundel's possessions were seized by the Crown; the estates of Bromfeld and Yale, Chirk, the Hundred of Oswestry and the County of Flint were all added to the County of Chester and at the Michaelmas Parliament the county was raised to the status of a 'principality'. The men of Richard's bodyguard were granted offices within the old Arundel estates: the custody of Oswestry was granted to Sir Robert de Legh; Chirk castle to Peter Dutton; Shrawardine castle to Thomas Beeston; Holt castle to Richard Cholmondeley; Richard Doddington became parker of Eyton; John Cholmondeley became forester of Bromfeld and Yale; Thomas Beeston parker of Shrawardine; and Sir John Mascy of Puddington was appointed steward of Hawarden. One of Richard's closest aides, Sir William Bagot, was appointed steward and surveyor of the Arundel lordships.

In January 1398, a Parliament was held at Shrewsbury and the whole of Richard's court moved north and the King visited his new 'principality'. At that Parliament, Henry Bolinbroke, the Duke of Hereford and Earl of Derby, accused Thomas Mowbray, Duke of Norfolk, of treason. The outcome was to be settled by a joust between the two which was to take place at Norwich, however, it was stopped at the last minute and Richard banished both men from the country, Hereford for ten years and Norfolk for life. At some time prior to his banishment Mowbray was confined at Windsor Castle for, on 15 April 1398, Sir Richard Craddock, 'the King's knight', was ordered to go to the constable of the castle and to take Mowbray to London, deliver him to the Lord Mayor and then to have him kept in the prison known as the 'Wardrobe' until his impeachment. John Kingsley of Nantwich had been one of Mowbray's esquires whilst he served as Justiciar of Chester and North Wales but he presumably survived his master's downfall.

On 20 July 1398, Roger Mortimer, Earl of March, the King's lieutenant in Ireland, was slain at the battle of Kelliston during an insurrection led by a rebel named McMorrough. On hearing of the news Richard planned a further visit to the country to avenge his cousin's death. Before departing for Ireland he named his heir as Edmund, Earl of March - the dead man's son.

Richard announced that he needed 2,000 Cheshire archers to accompany him and in an effort to recruit such a large force he visited the county. By October he was back in London from where he issued a Royal Warrant to authorise the payment of 4,000 marks (£2,666 13s 4d) to the people of Cheshire who had been injured at the battle of Radcot Bridge. The money was handed to Robert de Legh, the sheriff of the county, by the Treasurer of England, William Scrope, at Chester Castle on 16 October 1398. The payments went to 114 men who had been injured; the largest proportion of the money going to the men of the Macclesfield Hundred and the least of those of Nantwich. No doubt the payments helped the recruitment campaigns.

Early in 1399, on 24 February, Richard issued commands to the county administrators that all men between the ages of sixteen and sixty should be arrayed outside Watergate, Chester, ready for inspection on the morrow of the Ascension (9 May); from there those selected were to be conveyed to Burton and Denwall on Wirral for embarkation to Ireland. The following officers were commissioned to raise archers: Sir Richard Venables, William Brereton and Thomas Grosvenor had to raise eighty archers from the Northwich hundred; Sir John Mascy of Tatton, Sir William Legh, Peter Dutton, Sir John Pulford, William Stanley, Sir Richard Winnington, Sir John Haukeston, Sir Thomas Fouleshurst of Edlaston, Richard Vernon, William Venables of Bollin, Laurence Fytton, William Siddington, Hugh Browe, Phillip Egerton and John Egerton; all had similar commission respecting the other hundreds of the county. By 15 May Sir John Pulle and William Stanley were replaced by Vivian Foxwist and John de Litherland to lead their sixty archers, as Pulle and Stanley were under arrest for some reason.

In the spring the expedition got under way and the following were granted letters of protection: Thomas de Beeston, John Beeston de Tiverton, Laurance Fytton de Gawsworth, Sir John d'Arderne, David Bostock de Churton, Sir Hugh Browe, Richard Bruen, Simon Belot, Alexander de Cotton, William de Crue de Sandbach, Sir Thomas Danyers, Sir Thomas Fouleshurst, William Mascy, Richard Newton, William le Rotour de Kingsley, Richard Vernon, Thomas Venables of Frodsham, Reginald Wickstead, and Thomas de Wilbraham. Ten knights, 110 men-at-arms and 900 archer went from Cheshire to Ireland - half the number Richard had originally required.

* * *

On 3 February 1399 John of Gaunt, the Duke of Lancaster, died: his heir was the exiled Henry of Bolinbroke. Being an exile his estates were forfeit to the Crown and Richard had them divided up between his friends and supporters. Henry, a grandson of Edward III decided to re-enter England and to claim his inheritance, if necessary by force. In July he landed at Ravenspur in north-east England with a small army and began to march towards London.

King Richard had left the care of the realm to his trusted advisors, Bagot, Bushy and Green; the first of whom held lands in Cheshire including the revenues of Middlewich. On entering England Henry of Lancaster gathered a great deal of support; Henry Percy, Earl of Northumberland, Ralph Neville, Earl of Westmorland and the King's uncle, and the Duke of York all pledged themselves to Henry's cause. Although initially it was Henry's intention to take only what was his by inheritance by the time he reached London he was seeking the Crown. He no doubt considered Richard's choice of heir distasteful in view of the fact that the Mortimers were descended of Edward III through a female line, whereas both he and his uncle, York, were descended of a male line and had a better claim to the throne. Having started an insurrection against the King it was a matter of 'all or nothing'.

Richard's three courtiers were powerless to stop Henry's advance and fled from London to Bristol. Bushy and Green surrendered to Henry and were executed. Bagot flew to loyal Cheshire, no doubt to rally some defence, but he was caught and also executed. From

London and Bristol Henry marched to Chester to await Richard's return from Ireland. Hearing of his cousin's invasion Richard sent the Earl of Aumarle, son to the Duke of York, to North Wales with a large force, whilst he went to South Wales.

> *...He landed at Wales havyng attendynge upon hym at the same tyme seaven valient and generous esquires of the countie of Chester, by name John de Leigh de Boothes, Thomas Cholmondeley, Ralph DavenDorte, Adam Bostocke, John Downe, Thomas Beeston and Thomas Holford, and every one of these had the command of several companies especellie chosen out for the keepinge of the King's person in safetie..*

As one might expect the Earl of Aumarle deserted Richard's cause and joined his father. Richard had no choice but to submit to Henry, return the Duchy to him and to name him his heir. He met Lancaster at Flint castle, by which time his army had deserted him, and all he had left was his personal bodyguard - the men of the white hart. From Flint the King was escorted to Chester Castle and thence to London, arriving in the capital on 2 September. The Parliament sitting at Michaelmas, free of being surrounded by the Cheshire guard, found Richard unfit to govern and deposed him in favour of mighty Lancaster. From 30 September 1399, the Lancastrian dynasty ruled England.

* * *

References for Chapter Nine

Much of the information regarding the recruitment of the bodyguard has come from the *Calender of Recognizonce Rolls of the Palatinate of Chester*, 36th Report of the Deputy Keeper of the Public Records. *Foedera* and *Froissart's Chronicles* have again been consulted. A number of contemporary sources have been used for the critical references to the 'guard'. James L. Gillespie, B.A. Ph.D., wrote an excellent paper entitled 'Richard II's Cheshire Archers', printed in Vol. 125 of *Transactions of the Historic Society of Lancashire and Cheshire.*

* * *

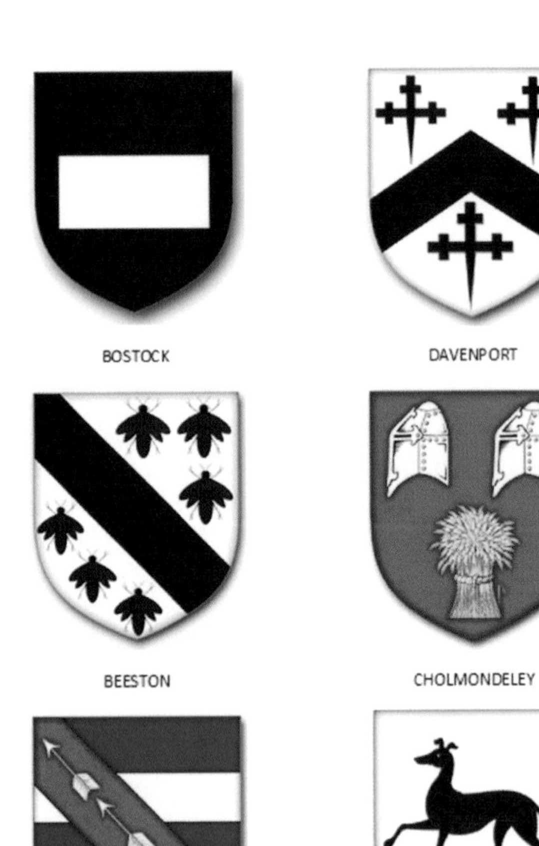
BOSTOCK
DAVENPORT
BEESTON
CHOLMONDELEY
DONE
HOLFORD

10. CHESHIRE'S REBELLION

The men of Cheshire had been on the losing side as they had enjoyed Richard's patronage but now they felt fear, anxiety and uncertainty. Members of Richard's guard went into hiding and became lawless bands, robbing and murdering Lancastrian supporters in Cheshire and the neighbouring counties.

On 23 January 1399, King Henry IV issued a general pardon to the people of Cheshire. A total of twenty-six were considered too dangerous and were exempt: the two sons of Robert Aldersey, Thomas Beeston, David Brayne, David Bostock of Churton, Nicholas Bulkeley, Thomas de Cholmondeley, Hugh de Cholmondeley, John de Cholmondeley of Broxton, William Clayton, William Coke, chaplain of Nantwich, Thomas Cottingham, Robert son of John Davenport of Bramhall, David Dodd of Edge, John Done of Utkinton, Thomas Holford, Thomas de Kelsall, John de Legh of Booths, Gilbert de Legh, William Mascy of Altringham, William Mascy of Knutsford, Robert de Overton, William Rotor, Roger de Salghall priest of Acton, Richard de Warburton, and Sir Richard de Winnington. From the list two names appear to be missing as all bar two of the captains of Richard's bodyguard are listed. The two missing men are Adam de Bostock and Ralph de Davenport, yet Adam's cousin is mentioned as is Ralph's cousin. The two men must therefore have become reconciled earlier on, probably soon after the Michaelmas Parliament, or at Henry's coronation on 13 October.

Despite the loyalty shown by the county to Richard, a few men were far-sighted enough to realise the outcome and rode to meet Henry at Shrewsbury. Two Cheshire men even rode with King Henry to Flint Castle where Richard was taken prisoner: these were Sir John and Sir Richard Legh - members of a family of divided loyalties. They were descended of earlier generations of the Venables family who had changed their name to Legh but kept the family's shield of arms of two silver bars against a blue background with subtle differences. Sir Piers de Legh of Adlington was executed on 10 August - his head was then placed on a spike above the Eastgate at Chester. John de Legh of Booths was exempted from the general pardon. Sir Richard Venables was a loyal supporter of the unfortunate King and at the time of Henry's landing was serving in Ireland. His brother William was a supporter of Lancaster's invasion and as a reward for his loyalty to Henry was given the title of Constable of Chester Castle.

By June 1400 Henry IV felt secure enough in his kingdom to mount an expedition against Scotland and confident enough to raise troops in Cheshire. During the next month an army of 13,000, of whom 11,000 were archers, marched to Scotland. The contingent from the 'rebel' county numbered 500: Macclesfield Hundred sent 100 archers with Sir Robert de Legh of Adlington and Ralph Davenport; Bucklow, 103 with Sir John Mascy of Tatton and Sir John Savage; Northwich, 60 with Sir Richard de Venables, baron of Kinderton; Broxton, 60 with Richard Cholmondelegh; Nantwich, 60 with Sir Richard de Vernon, baron of Shipbrook; Eddisbury, 60 with Sir Richard de Winnington; and finally the Wirral sent 40 with John de Poole. A number of persons known for their loyalty to the last king had therefore now found favour with the new regime. The expedition gained nothing apart fro burning and pillaging the border region. In September the army returned home and whilst journeying south they learned of a rebellion in Wales: Owen Glyn Dwr, an esquire of noble Welsh lineage, had assumed the title of Prince of Wales, a title held by Henry of Monmouth, Henry IV's eldest son.

The Welsh revolt scored well in its first year and reduced English influence in Wales considerably: by 1402 Owen had effective control of the Welsh people. The revolt had started over a feud in North Wales between Owen and his neighbour Lord Grey of Ruthin concerning certain lands but this soon flared into a rebellion covering all of Wales. The policing of the Principality was left to Prince Henry aided by Henry Percy, known as Hotspur, the heir to the Earldom of Northumberland and Justice of North Wales. Another of Prince Henry's aides was Edmund Mortimer, uncle to the Earl of March, who had been named heir by Richard II. In an attempt to put the rebellion down an invasion was planned by the King but he was beaten back at a savage battle in Herefordshire. During the battle Edmund Mortimer was taken prisoner and held by Glyn Dwr for ransom. King Henry refused to pay the money and consequently Mortimer went over to the Welsh side and called upon his retainers to do likewise; Mortimer even married Owen Glyn Dwr's daughter to cement their alliance.

Hotspur returned to the northern marches in 1402 to defend them against Scottish incursions and in that year he won a decisive victory over the Scots at Homildon Hill, which made the name of Hotspur famous throughout the country. Despite their power the Percy family were becoming dissatisfied with England's new King: they had helped him to the throne, yet received nothing in return; they had helped him in Wales yet they had received no payment; Hotspur had taken the Earl of Douglas prisoner at the battle at Homildon Hill but the King had had him released without ransom; and King Henry refused to ransom Mortimer, Hotspur's brother in law. In view of their many differences with the Crown, the Earl of Northumberland and his son sided with the Welsh cause. A conspiracy was hatched and by the Treaty of Partition they agreed to overthrow King Henry and split England up with Mortimer ruling southern England and the Percies the north, leaving Owen to rule Wales.

Hotspur travelled to Cheshire to recruit those still loyal to the name of Richard II and the Earls of March. He announced that Richard was alive and in hiding in Chester (he had in fact died at the turn of the century at Pontefract Castle whilst a prisoner there). Hotspur also told the people of Cheshire that Richard would show himself to his loyal subjects at Sandiway; the badge of the 'white hart' was distributed to those who were recruited and once again the men of Cheshire wore 'the livery of the stag'.

Meanwhile Henry IV was planning to invade Wales with his son who was garrisoned at Shrewsbury. The King collected his forces at Burton on Trent where, despite the rising in Cheshire, a number of Cheshire men were in the royal army: John Calveley (a nephew of the famous Hugh), Thomas Maisterson of Nantwich, John Mascy of Pudington, Laurence Fytton, and Robert Fouleshurst. On hearing of the conspiracy Henry marched to Lichfield and thence to Shrewsbury where he intended to meet his son.

Of course Richard did not show himself at Sandiway but still the Cheshire men followed Hotspur against the King whom they considered a usurper. From Sandiway the small army marched to Nantwich where they burned the home of Thomas Maisterson. Hotspur and his retinue marched to Stafford to meet his uncle, Thomas Percy, Earl of Worcester, whose lieutenant was Sir Richard Craddock of Nantwich. The 'rebels' marched towards Shrewsbury intent upon taking the town and taking the young Prince and thus opening a bridge into Wales. The Cheshire men marched by way of Prees, Shropshire whilst Henry Hotspur and his uncle marched by way of Newport and High Ercall.

Of the 5,000 'rebels', about 700 were Cheshire men amongst whom, Adam de Bostock had a command, as had Sir John Poole and Sir William Stanley, who agreed to lead twenty four lances and forty-eight archers (about 120 men); Sir Hugh Browe also led a company, as did Sir Richard Venables and Sir Richard Vernon.

King Henry and his party arrived at Shrewsbury on 19 July, a matter of hours before Hotspur. The following day offers of peace were made by the King to the rebels but to no avail. The army led by Glyn Dwr failed to appear as it could not cross the river Severn. On the morning of 21 July, Henry IV sent Laurence Fytton to guard the river Dee against any crossing the Welsh might make there and then rode out of Shrewsbury to meet the 'rebels'.

The site of the battle gave no advantage to either side. The countryside was flat save for a very gentle slope to the north. The field of battle lay between the manors of Albright Hussey and the main road north out of Shrewsbury, some three miles away. The gradual sloping ground was selected by Hotspur for his position and on it he placed his archers.

During the initial stages of the battle the Cheshire bowmen made good use of their weapon; the effect was devastating but unfortunately it was not continued as they were short of arrows and soon ran out. The King's archers were better supplied and able to keep a more constant fire upon their enemy. Hotspur fought in the thick of the battle trying to cut his way through to the royal standard and the King. However, the king was not with his standard and had cunningly dressed a number of knights with the royal arms. The Earl of Douglas is said to have remarked, 'Never did I see so many Kings arise one on the neck of another'. In the thick of the battle Hotspur was slain and with his death the battle came to an end - the 'rebels' had lost.

The battle, which was fought on a hot Saturday afternoon, lasted about four hours and left a very heavy death toll. Estimates of the casualties are as high as 1,600 'royalists' dead and 3,000 wounded, with 5,000 'rebels' dead. Of the latter who died on the field of battle or in the ensuing chase, 200 were Cheshire knights and esquires; Sir John Mascy and Thomas Beeston being two. Some Cheshire men on the Royalist side also died; two of them were Sir John Calveley and Sir John Mascy of Puddington who had been newly dubbed knights by the King.

Along with Thomas Percy, Venables and Vernon were taken prisoner. All three were executed at the Market Cross in Shrewsbury and Percy's head was sent to London to be displayed on London Bridge. The bodies of the barons of Kinderton and Shipbrook were taken by the sheriff of Shropshire to the mayor of Chester so that they might be displayed on the gates of the City, 'for so long as they last', to deter other would-be rebels; a part of Hotspur's body was also displayed at Chester.

Some of the Cheshire men forfeited their estates for their parts in the rebellion. John Mainwaring, the 'King's servant', received the lands of Sir Hugh Browe; Sir John de Stanley, the 'King's knight', received the lands of sir John de Poole, Sir William Stanley, and others. The lands of Robert de Leftwich were granted to William de Kirkby, a 'yeoman of the chamber' to the Prince of Wales, should Leftwich continue in his rebellious ways. An order of confiscation was issued against Adam de Bostock though, however, it seems that it was never executed.

The Kingsleys of Nantwich were espoused to the Percy cause. John senior, parson of Pulford, and his son John of Nantwich, were at the battle. The parson was wounded and his son fled to his mother's house at Chester. As a result, on 22 July, a grant was issued to Mathew de Swettenham of all lands rents and goods which belonged to John Kingsley 'forfeit to the King, on account of the rebellion of the said John Kingsley, because he had been armed with Henry Percy in the battle of Shrewsbury against the King'. The property of Petronilla, wife of John Kingsley senior, was forfeit too, 'because she knowingly received [the younger] John into her house'. The rebellious priest went back to his living at Pulford where he remained until his death in 1406.

On 25 July the King granted his son, the Earl of Chester, full power to punish the 'rebels', or to treat for pardon on receipt of a suitable fine. By November, 3,000 marks had been collected in payments for fines from such people as Sir John de Poole (who then received his lands back from Stanley), James de Poole, John Kingsley and his sons, Adam Bostock, William Stanley and his son, Sir Peter Dutton, Sir Robert de Legh, and Richard Mascy. Thomas Beeston had been slain but Prince Henry showed compassion to his family by pardoning his widow and granting her a pension.

A number of Cheshire men who remained loyal to the King were rewarded by his son; Sir John Stanley became steward of the King's household, John Mainwaring was appointed Sheriff of Chester and Laurence Fytton was appointed to an official post.

The battle of Shrewsbury is dealt with by Shakespeare in *King Henry IV, Part One*; in his play the author uses Sir Richard Vemon as one of the characters, often entering the stage with Thomas Percy the Earl of Westmorland. The playwright also states that Thomas Percy and Vernon were taken before the King after the battle and that the King ordered their executions, 'Bear Worcester to the death, and Vernon too: Other offenders we will pause upon.'

The battle saw the end of revolt against the house of Lancaster. In later years the men of Cheshire served the King and his son well and served with distinction at the battle of Agincourt, where once again Cheshire bowmen ranked supreme and were a vital part in the victory. Cheshire men through their military prowess served both the houses of Plantagenet and Lancaster well indeed.

* * *

References for Chapter Ten

Various contemporary chronicles. *Calendar of Recognizance Rolls* and other rolls

* * *

MAISTERSON

BULKELEY

LEGH OF ADLINGTON

VENABLES

WINNINGTON

MAINWARING

11. MONUMENTS TO THE PAST

The end of Richard's reign saw the physical decline of some of Cheshire's heroes. On St. George's Day, 23 April, 1393 Sir Hugh Calveley died. At Bunbury, where Sir Hugh had made improvements to the church of St Boniface and founded a college and chantry for a master and six priests, a marvelous tomb chest with a recumbent effigy of the great warrior was erected to his memory. Froissart in his chronicles hints at an illegitimate child of Sir Hugh's, for in recording the departure of the Earl of Buckingham from Calais in 1361, he mentions: "Hughlyn Caverell, bastarde" and says he rode with Sir Hugh, and Sir Hugh Browe. 'Cavarell' was one of his styles for spelling Calverley. Although Sir Hugh may not have had any legitimate children, his surname exists in the county today, as do the names of so many of the Cheshire heroes.

Sir Robert died on 15 August 1407. He, like his kinsman, was a benefactor of the church. In 1385 he founded a college and a hospital for a master and six priests to cater for thirteen poor men and women in Pontefract, Yorkshire, the birthplace of his wife. The hospital and college were known as 'Knolles' Almshouses'; though closed at the time of the Dissolution of the Monasteries they were revived and exist today. In 1398 Sir Robert rebuilt and endowed the bridge and chantry at Rochester, Kent. He also had the churches of Sculthorpe and Harpley, Norfolk, rebuilt and gave donations to the Carmalite monks at Whitefriars, London. Sir Robert's munificence is shown in his two wills. By the first will dated 21 October 1399 he left his London property to the benefit of the hospital at Pontefract. The executors of this will included his cousin Hugh Browe and Richard Seymour, prior of Norton Priory. The second will, dated 20 May 1404, left money for masses to be heard in various churches and 100s for the church at Malpas - was this the church of his baptism and boyhood? Sir Robert died at his manor of Sculthorpe and his body was then removed to Whitefriars, London, for burial. A few days later his wife also died and she too was taken to lie beside him. The church at Whitefriars unfortunately no longer stands.

Unfortunately there is no memorial to Sir Robert Knolles. However, there is an image on a boss in Norwich Cathedral said to be of Sir Robert and Lady Knolles: Robert and his wife are shown kneeling with a representation of the Trinity between them. One of the paintings in an edition of Froissart's chronicles depicts him on horseback leading an army. Also, on the postern tower of Bodiam Castle, Suffolk, Sir Robert's shield of arms is carved as a mark of respect to the great warrior. The castle builder was Sir Edward Dalyngrigge who served in Knolles company between 1367 and 1377 making for himself immense riches by which he was able to begin building the castle in 1385. That one of Robert's subordinates could afford such an extravagance perhaps says a great deal about Robert's own fortunes.

* * *

We are fortunate in this county in having some excellent effigies which bear witness to the times, and they clearly show the form of armour worn by those warriors.

The earliest effigy is that to Sir William Boydell which lies at the parish church of Grappenhall, near Warrington. Much of this effigy has been repaired and some of historical detail has gone, nevertheless the effigy shows Sir William wearing a crude form of plate armour. The limbs are cased in strips of plate which are overlapped and riveted together on a leather foundation. His jupon is clearly marked with his arms. At his left side he had a shield which is supported by a thin strap which hangs from the right shoulder and he has a simple sword belt with a circular buckle. The warrior is depicted in a restless pose with his legs crossed and his hands grasping the sword and scabbard as though ready to draw it in action.

In Cheshire the best known effigy is that to Sir Hugh Calveley in the chancel at Bunbury church. He is shown in a relaxed pose with his hands together on his breast in prayer. He wears a complete harness of plate: his limbs are encased in plate, the feet in 'lobster tail' shoes of plate, his hands are encased in plate gauntlets. The camail made from chain mail is clearly carved and on his head he has the typical conical helmet. His armour is enriched with carved borders, especially the helmet, in the way many rich nobles followed the practice of enriching their armour with gold or silver. The arms of the Calveley family are carved on the jupon and the three calves are still quite clear. The hem of the jupon is scalloped and stops short to reveal the skirt of mail. Sir Hugh's head rests on his great helm, which bears his calf's head crest, which he would have worn at tournaments or on ceremonial occasions. It is not thought that Hugh's body lies beneath the memorial - in fact we do not know for sure where he was buried. The tomb chest was once adorned with paintings of shields depicting the arms of both Sir Hugh and Sir Robert Knolles - so did Sir Robert commission the monument in honour of his kinsman and comrade-in-arms?

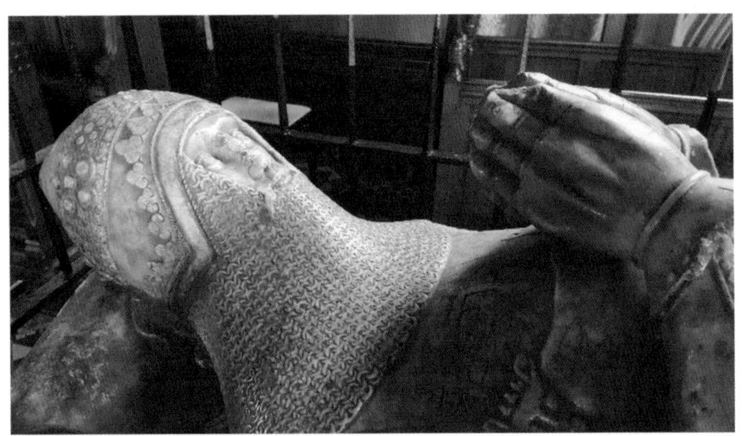

The effigy of Sir Hugh Calveley in Bunbury church

At the castle of Mont Orgueil, Jersey, there is a magnificent steel statue to Sir Hugh mounted on a horse in recognition of his time as Governor of the Channel Isles.

Four other effigies bear witness to this glorious, chivalric period of Cheshire's history and all show armour similar to Sir Hugh's. At Acton, in the Church of St. Mary, there lies the effigy of Sir William Mainwaring of Baddiley and Peover who died in 1399. Around his neck he wears a collar of 'S's which indicates his allegiance to the House of Lancaster. The 'torse', which was used to create padding when the great helm was lowered over the pointed 'bascinet', is carved to show enrichment of jewels and pearls. On the front of his helmet the words "JESV NAZERENVS REX" are carved. His arms comprising of two red bars on a white background are carved on the jupon. The crest of an ass's head is mounted on the great helm.

The effigy of Sir William Mainwaring in Acton church

Sir Robert Fouleshurst lies at the church of St. Bertoline at Barthomley. He died in the early years of the reign of Henry IV, and around his neck he wears the Lancastrian collar of S's. In 1387 Sir Ralph Davenport died and his recumbent effigy lies at Astbury. In 1410 John Mainwaring of Peover passed on and his remains lie beneath his effigy at Over Peover. In the parish church of Nantwich there is a damaged effigy to the memory of Sir Richard Craddock. On his breast his arms 'Argent, on a chevron Azure, three garbs Or', are carved. His feet rest on a lion and his head on a great helm, which carries the lamb's head crest.

The effigy of Sir John Mainwaring in Over Peover church

The many effigies of the county bear witness to its military and chivalric past. Throughout the reigns of Henry IV and his son, the legendary Henry V, Cheshire men constantly served in France, especially at the famous battle of Agincourt. Loyalties were divided in the bitter struggle known as the Wars of the Roses and within the county brother fought brother, cousin was against cousin - a foretaste of the Civil War of two hundred years later.

The effigy of Sir Robert Fouleshurst in Barthomley church

As the fourteenth century began England was a young nation beginning to forge her influence in Europe. The victories won in France established her as a superior military power and earned a reputation which for centuries never waned. The successes at Crecy and Poitiers served as bywords of military skill and have been something of an inspiration to the British Army ever since. The fact that the men of Cheshire played such an important role should fill the modern Cheshire man with pride.

* * *

BIBLIOGRAPHY

Various documents preserved in the British Museum, The Public Record Office (PRO) and the Cheshire Record Office (CRO) have been used.

PRINTED RECORD SOURCES

Register of Edward the Black Prince, 4 vols, published by the Deputy Keeper of the Public Records (1930-1933)
Calendar of Close Rolls, 45 vols, PRO (1892-1954)
Calendar of Fine Rolls 22 vols, PRO (1911-1963)
Calendar of Plea Rolls 70 vols, PRO (1891-1982)
Foedera, conventines, literae et acta publica, ed. T. Rymer , 7 vols (1816-1869)

* * *

NARRATIVE AND LITERARY SOURCES

Baker, Geoffrey le, *Chronicon*, ed. & trans. by E.M. Thompson (1889).
Bel, Jean, *Chroniques*, ed. J. Viard and E. Déprez, 2 vols (1904-5)
Chandos Herald, *Life of the Black Prince*, ed. D.B. Tyson (1975)
Froissart Jean, *The Chronicles of Jean Froissart*, trans. Lord Berners, ed. G.C. McCauley (1910)
Knighton, Henry, *Chronicle, 1337-1376*, ed. G.H.Martin (1955)
Gray, Sir Thomas of Heton, *Scalacronica*, ed., J. Stevenson (1836)
Walsingham, Thomas, *Historia Anglicana* ed. H.T.Riley, 2 vols (1863-4)

* * *

OTHER SOURCES AND FURTHER READING

Armitage-Smith, S.,*John of Gaunt*, (1904)
Burne, A.H., *The Crecy War* (1955)
Cole, H., *The Black Prince* (1976)
Driver, J.T., *Cheshire in the later Middle Ages* (1971)
Emerson, B., *The Black Prince* (1976)
Fowler, K.,*The King's Lieutenant, Henry of Grosmont, Duke of Lancaster,*

1310-1361 (1969)
Hewitt, H.J., *Medieval Cheshire* (1929)
Hewitt, H.J., *The Black Prince's expeditions of 1355-57* (1958)
Hewitt, H.J., *The organization of War under Edward III, 1338-62* (1966)
Hewitt, H.J., *Cheshire Under the Three Edwards* (1967)
Hutchinson, H.J., *The Hollow Crown: a Life of Richard II* (1961)
McKisack, M., *The Fourteenth Century* (1963)
Ormerod, G., *The History of the Palatine of Chester* 3 vols. ed. T. Helsby (1899)
Steel, A., *Richard II (1962)*
Stone, B., *Sir Gawain and the Green Knight* (1974)
Sumption, J., *Trial by Battle: The Hundred Years War, Volume 1*(1999)
Sumption, J., *Trial by Fire: The Hundred Years War, Volume 2*(2001)
Sumption, J., *Divided Houses: The Hundred Years War, Volume 3*(2002)
Uden, G., *A Dictionary of Chivalry* (1968)
Wrottesley, G., *Crecy and Calais* (1898)

APPENDICES

The following lists include those people who were born, lived or held lands in Cheshire. In most instances the spellings are as found in documents of the time. The appendices covering the various campaigns are not complete as to list the many hundreds would be a long and tedious task and beyond the intended scope of this work; however, those names easily found in records of rewards and amongst the letters of protection have been listed and give a good impression of the numbers and names of Cheshire men involved at various times. The abbreviation Kt. = knight

* * *

APPENDIX ONE

The names of those who served in the Crecy campaign and siege of Calais in 1346 and 1341.

Giles d'Arderne, Kt.
James d'Audeley of Helegh, Kt.
Richard Baskervylle, Kt.
William Brereton, Kt.
Alymer de la Brette, Kt.
John de Bulkelegh
William de Bulkelegh de Alprham, junior
Thomas de Betteleye
John le Bruyn
Peter de Bunbury
Roger de Cheyney, Kt.
Thomas Crue
Hugh, son of David Crue
Wiiliam Crue
Thomas Daniers, Kt.
John Delves. Kt.
John Davenport, Kt.
John Gryffyth, Kt.
John Gandy
Edmund de Goghull
John Hyde, Kt.
Walter Hewitt, Kt.
Thomas Haulton
John de Haukeston, Kt.
William Felton, Kt.
Robert de Legh de Adlington
Hamon Mascy, Kt.
John Mascy, parson of Sefton
Richard Mascy
Thomas Mascy
Randolph de Munshull
Ralph de Oldyngton
Henry Praers
Adam de Sharyngton
Richard de Stapleton, Kt.
Hamon le Strange

John le Strange, de Whitchurch, Kt.
Richard de Stanleye, Kt.
William de Tabley
Warine de Trussell. Kt.
William de Trussell de Cblestone. Kt.
John Trussell, Kt.
Alexander de Venables, Kt.
Richard de Venables. Kt.
Nicholas de Vernon
Alexander Wasteneys
Malcolm Wasteneys de Tixhall. Kt.
Thomas Wasteneys
Peter son of John de Wetenhale de Munshull
Peter de Wetenhale, Kt.
John de Whiston, Kt.
Richard de Worleston
John son of Robert de St. Peirre
Ralph de Stathum

APPENDIX TWO

The Cheshire men known to have served in Gascony, in the years between 1355 and 1357; those known to have been at the battle of Poitiers are marked with an asterisk *.

Adam de Acton*, Richard de Acton, Robert de Acton, William de Acton, Roger Amory, William de Apulton*, Thomas d'Arderne, Robert son of Peter de Astell* James d'Audeley, Kt.*

William de Bacton, Hamon de Bagley, John de Bagley, Thomas de Baguley de Knutsford, sen.*, William de Bechyngton*, Thomas de Belgrave* Robert Benet, Ralph Berchels, Adam Broadhewer*, William de Bollyngton, John Boydell, Robert Bolt*, Roger de Bosedon*, Adam de Bostok*, Nicholas de Bostok, Robert Bowden, John le Bower, Thomas le Brett, Ralph de Bredbury*, William Bridyn, Robert Brun, Adam le Bryn, William le Bryn, Robert le Bryn de Stapleford,

William Calday, Geoffrey Carpenter, William de Caryngton, Kt., Alan Cheyne, Kt.*, William de Chorley, John de Cotton, Richard le Crouther, Yevon de Crouther, John Chandos Kt.*

John Danyers Kt.*, William Davy de Stuthbache, Thomas Doune, Nicholas del Dounes*, William del Dounes, William Dodd, Thomas Donne de Crowton, John de Eton, Thomas Elensone, John Fairchild, Thomas Felton Kt., John Fytoun Kt.*, John son of Hugh Fytoun*, William Flecchere*, John Fog, Thomas Frodsham*, Thomas son of John Frodsham*

Roger Gille, Hugh de Golbourne, William de Golbourne Kt.*, John Gryffyn Kt., Simon de Grimsditch*, Robert Grosvenor Kt.*

Roger de Handforth, John Harding, John Hargreave, Thomas de Haselyngton*, Robert Herthull, John Hyde Kt.*, Richard Hikedon*, Robert Hikedon, William de Holford*, Roger de Honford*, Robert de Hoton, William de Huxley*, Ralph de Halsale

David ap Jacke, William Jane*, John Jodrell*, Randolphe de Kelsalle*, John Ketel, Peter de Kirkeby

William Malpas, Hamon de Mascy*, Richard de Mascy*, Robert son of Benet de Molyngton*, Adam de Mottram, Hugh Millington, Randolph de Mobberley Kt., Hugh de Mottram, Phillip le Mou, Hugh de Mulyngton

Henry Neston, Robert Neville Kt.*, Robert de Newbold, William de Newton*, John de Northley, Peter de Northley

John de Overton

Robert Parkyn, Hugh 1e Paver, David Pynk*

Thomas de Raby, John de Rosnregrene, Thomas de Rouley*

John de Samesfeld*, Richard Savage, William Scot, David Seys de Egge, Richard le Sergeant*, Thomas Sharp, Hugh de Siddington*, Roger Simondsonet, Roger le Smyth, William Spark, Hugh Starkey, John son of Richard Starkey of Stretton*, William de Stewhalle, William de Stockport*, Randolph de Stoke*, John de Stockton, John de Swettenham*, Richard de Swettenham, Roger de Swettenham, Thomas de Stathum, William de Stretton

Hamon le Tailour de Whatcroft, John ie Tailour de Whatcroft, William de Thenewall*, David de Thornley*, William Trussell Kt.*, John de Tuwe, John de Trvembrook, Thomas de Twembrook

APPENDIX THREE

Some of the Cheshire men who served with the Prince in Aquitaine in 1369.

James d'Audeley Kt., Geoffrey le Boidell, William de Brereton Kt., Hugh le Browe Kt., Richard Bulkelegh, Hugh de Coton, Robert D'anyel, Thomas Duncalfe, Laurence Dutton Kt., Vivian de Foxwist, John de Frodsham, Richard Fytton Kt., John Gryfin , Robert Grosvenor Kt., William de Hilton, William de Hulme, Thomas de Legh, William de Legh Kt., William de Legh, Richard Manley, John de Mascy, Robert de Pilkington, William de Praers, Thomas Seint Pierre, William del Slene, Robert de Toft, William de Tranmere, Ralph Vernon Kt., Richard de Vernon, Richard de Wynyngton.

APPENDIX FOUR

Cheshire men and their commanders who served in the Reims campaign, 1359.

Men-at-arms

James d'Audeley Kt., Richard Baskervyle Kt., John Chandos Kt., John Danyel Kt., William Caryngton Kt., Thomas Dutton, John Fitoun Kt., Thomas Fogg Kt., Robert Fouleshurst Kt., Robert Knol1ys Kt., William Golbourne Kt., John Gryffyn Kt., John Hyde Kt., Robert de Legh the son, William de Legh, Hamon de Mascy, Richard de Mascy, Ralph de Modberlegh Kt., Thomas de Stathum, Thomas de Swinnerton Kt., Geoffrey de Wereburton Kt.

Archers in the retinue of Sir Bartholemew de Burghersh

Thomas Baudrick, William de Bermyncham, Thomas le Fisshere, William Martyn, Hamon son of Thomas Mascy, Hugh le Paver, William le Pevere, John Parour, Thomas le Parker de Newhalle, Thomas de Radilegh, Roger de Roulegh, William de Shere, Thomas Smith de Munshull, Robert son of William Starky, Richard de Syndyngton, John de Venables, Robert de Waryngton, Randolph de Wevere, Hugh de Wirhale, Richard de Wynyngton

Archers in the retinue of Sir John de Wengefeld

Robert Bolt, John de Berewyck, Thomas Sharp, William de Wynyngton,

Archers in the retinues of other nobles, including the Prince

Roger de Brescy (in the retinue of the Earl of March); Richard de Brome, Huwet Dawe, John de Drokenfeld, William de Copenhale, John de Holyngworth, William Janny (in the retinue of John Danyel Kt.); John de Swettenham.

Archers who fell sick in the month of October 1359, and did not make the journey. Alongside each, in brackets, is the name of the captain who certified the man's condition.

John Broun (Mobberley), Hugh de Dounes (Legh), Edmund son of Philip d'Aldelym (Warburton), Hamon son of William de Hull (Warburton), Ralph de Hull (Warburton), John de Holm (Fitton), Thomas son of Richard Rosselyn (Fitton), Thomas Rosselyn (Fitton), Hugh le Vernon (Mobberley), Richard Taillour de

Shipbrook (Mobberley), William Gostre (Mobberley), John Swon (Mascy), Hugh Swon of H'lae (Mascy), John son of Richard Hardyng (Mobberley), Robert de Aiston (Legh, the son), Henry de Smyth de Stockport (Legh, the son), Gilbert Baret (Legh, he son), Philip Filkyn (Stathum), John de Haselyngton (Warburton), Adam Malbon (Warburton), Roger de Dutton (Dutton), William de Beriton (Dutton), Hugh Dagge (Dutton), Roger de Mortresheved (Daniel), John de Pottresheved (Daniel), William de Housebourne (Daniel), Roger Holdhed (Daniel), Richard son of Simon de Mottrum (Daniel), Robert Wither (Carrington), Roger Wilme (Carrington), Robert Pikeryng (Fitton), Oliver de Barlegh (Fitton), Thomas son of Thomas le Bryd (Golbourn), John Boyl (Golbourn), Robert de Mottrum (Daniel) Thomas de Assheton (Daniel)

APPENDIX FIVE

The following men were rewarded in compensation for their injuries, received at the battle of Radcot Bridge, in December 1387, together with the total payments for each Hundred. The names of those from Bucklow Hundred are not known: the hundred received £566 19s 10d.

Broxton Hundred: £220 2s 9¼d.

Ughtred de Huxlegh
Roger de Dytton
Thomas le Belewe
William de Caurthyn
William de Mulneton, Jun
Thomas Dod
Patrick de Huxegh
John de Congleton
John de Aldressey
John de Caurthyn
Robert Godemon, Sen
Robert Godernon, Jun
William le Warde, de Byberton
Hugh son of William Browe
Phillip de Broxton
Hugh de Massey
Jor' de Crue
Richard de Caldecot
Phillip de Hunsterton

Eddisbury Hundred: £356 15s 4¾d.

Richard de Wynyngton, Kt.
William de Venables de Troghford
Robert Danyell de Rydlegh
William le Rotour
Richard Done of Utkynton
Thomas Venables de Frodsham
William de Frodsham de Elton
Henry le Bruyn de Dunham

Thomas Water
John le Taillour de Thornton
Henry del Halle
Thomas, son of Richard de Thornton
Thomas Geegod
William le Vernon
Henry le Crouther
Thomas le Hopwode
Thomas Parson
John Gryffyn
Richard Spark
Randal de Mulneton

Macclesfield Hundred: £709 5s 1½d.

Peter de Legh
John de Legh de Macclesfield
Robert del Dounes
Reginald del Dounes
William de Sydyngton
Edmund Fytton
John de Leversage
John de Chorlegh
William Slegh
Robert Coulegh
Nicholas le Gardyner
John de Wakefeld
Stephen del Rowe
Thomas Nicholas
Thomas de Hurdesfeld
William Wylot
John de Oldefeld
Richard del Knolles

Nantwich Hundred: £183 8s 10¾d.

Richard le Vernoun
David le Saint Pierre
John de Kelshall
Roger Alkoc
John le Eyre
Roger le Wodewer
Richard le Rope

Thomas del Heath
Thomas le Praers
John del Castell
John le Crouth
John de Erdelegh
Thomas le Vernoun
Nicholas Willesone
John de Buyrton
Thomas de Sondebache
Roger de Stapeley
James le Vernoun

NORTHWICH HUNDRED: £218 4S 7¾D.

Richard de Morton
John le Littleover
Robert de Smethwyk
Robert Brothersone
Richard Gandy
Peter le Warde
William de Deys
William de Swettenham
Ralph de Somerford
Robert Proudglove
William Scot
Thomas Scaryot
Randal de Bradshagh
Thomas Devot
Richard Wilkynsone
Peter Dykensone
Adam de Smalwode
Thomas de Cudlesford
Henry le Serjant
Ralph de Radnore

WIRRAL HUNDRED: £411 16S 8D

John de Pulle Kt.
William de Stanley
Thomas de Hogh
John de Lytherland
John de Warewyk
William de Trauenroele

Gilbert Clegg
John de Bebyngton
William le Meols
David de Staney
William de Wilbram
John Coly
Thomas de Lee
Roger Trull
Robert Hopkynsone
Richard le Smyth
Robert Baumvill
Robert le Clerk
John de Holden
William Turfmes

APPENDIX SIX

A list of Cheshire men recruited by the King for his personal army and bodyguard. They were recruited between the years 1397 and 1398. The grants or appointments follow a similar style: *a grant of the livery of the Crown with 6d., a day for life*(or *during pleasure*); some are *appointed a yeoman of the livery of the Crown, with 6d., a day for life* (or *during pleasure*); and some are *appointed archers of the livery.* Some of the grants and appointments have a marginal notation *Sagittarius de Corona*(Archer of the Crown) and these have been listed separately.

The letters L and P indicate whether the grant is for life (L) or during the King's pleasure (P). The letters G, Y, and A indicate whether the person receives a simple grant of livery (G) or is appointed a yeoman (Y), or an archer (A).

Richard de Acton G.P.
John de Acton G.L
Robert de Aldecroft of Dunham Y.L
John. brother of Robt. de Aldecroft Y.L
Hamon, brother of Robt. de Aldecroft Y.L
William de Aldecroft G.L
John de Aldersey G.L
David de Alpraham G.L
Robert de Anderton G.P
Thomas Arnekoc G.L
Richard Ashton G.L
Thomas Ashton G.L

Thomas Balle Y.L
Randolph Baret Y.L
William Baret G.L
John Bate, archer of the Principality of Wales Y.L
Thomas Becheton A.L
Roger de Beeston G.L
Ralph de Bellew, archer the Principality of Wales Y.L
Richard Bennett of Nantwich A.L
Lawrence de Bentley G.L
Adam Berughby, archer of the Principality of Wales Y.L
John de Bickerstath, archer of Chester G.L

Hugh de Bickerton G.L
Hugh Byrd G.L
Roger de Birkenhead G.L
John de Blackenhall G.L
John de Bodhum A.L
Richard Boor of Thornton Y.L
David Bostock of Churton G.L
David son of David Bostock G.L
John son of David Bostock G.L
John Bostock of Worleston G.L
Thomas son of John Bostock G.L
Thomas son of Adam Bostock G.L
Thomas son of Wm. Bostock G.L
William Bostock G.L
Richard atte Boughey G.L
William Boydell G.L
Richard de Bradford Y.P
Roger de Bradford Y.P
John de Bradelegh A.L
Lawrence de Bradshagh G.L
David Brayn Y.L
Henry son of David Brayn Y.L
Thomas son of David Brayn Y.L
Henry son of Thomas Brayn Y.L
Henry Brayn Hodekynsone Y.L
Roger Brayn Y.L
William Brayne Y.L
Robert Bressy G.P
Roger de Bromley Y.L
Richard de la Bromford G.L
John Brok G.L
Robert Brotherson G.L
John Brownwynd Y.L
Peter Byrch, archer of Chester G.P
Henry Bryene od Dunham Y.L
Hugh Bulkeley G.L
Richard Bulkeley A.L
John son of Peter Bulkeley Y.L
John de Burton G.L

Thomas Davy A.L
Hugh Davy A.L
Adam Denys G.P
Richard Derplegh A.L
William de Deye A.L
William Dobyn. archer ol Chester Y.L
David Dodd G.L
William Dodd G.L
Richard Doddington Y.L
William Done of Kelsall G.L
Richard, brother of Wm. Done G.L
Thomas de Dounes G.P
Hugh le Draper archer of Chester G.L
Roger Drewery G.L
John Duncan G.L
John de Dokyngton A.L
John Dyseworth G.P
John son of John Dyseworthg. G.P

Hamo de Eton G.L

William Fairchild de Altringham G.L
Robert Fales, archer Y.L
William de Farrington G.L
William Ferror Y.L
Morgan Filkin G.L
John Fisch G.L
John Fischer G.L
William Forest G.P
Thomas Forester Y.L
Thomas Foster G.L
Thomas son of Hugh de Frodsham G.L

William Glaskerain G.P
Hugh Gleave G.P
John de Golbourne de Horton A.L
John de Golbourne de Bunbury G.L
Peter Goldstone G.L
William de Grafton G.L
Thomas del Grene, yeo archer of Chester A.L
Philip Grene Y.L

Richard de Grene Y.L
Richard Griffitson G.L
John Grimsditch G.L
William Grimsditch G.L

Thomas Harding A.L
Robert de Hasale G.L
John Hatton, clerc Y.L
William de Hatton A.L
Simon de Hatton A.L
Roger Hawarden Y.L
Thomas Haynson de Sandbach, yeo. Y.L
Nicholas Haynson G.L
Robert de Heth de Overton G.L
Thomas del Heth Y.L
Richard de Helegh A.L
Thomas Henshawe, archer of Wales Y.L
Thomas Hulgeave A.L
Patrick de Huxley G.L
William de Huxley G.L
William de Huyme G.L

John Keckwith Y.L
Richard de Keyslegh G.L
Robert Kinsey de Blackden G.L
Thomas Kinsey de Blackden G.L
William Kinsey de Blackden G.L
Gruff' de Kynerton G.L

John de Lancaster Y.L
John Lawrence A.L
Hugh de Lathom G.L
Hugh de Lawton, archer of Wales A.L
Randel de Lawton G.L
David de Lawton G.L
Richard Ledbeter G.L
John Leeche G.L
Stephen de Lene de Maxfield Y.L
Wiiliam Littleover G.L

John Mason Y.L
John Mason Y.L
John le Massey G.L
John Mascy Y.L
John Medewell G.L

Thomas de Newton G.L

Roger de Page G.L
Henry de Pynyngton A.L
William Plummer, archer of Chester Y.L
John son of Henry de Pulford A.L
William de Pullowe G.L

Richard Ridelegh A.L
John Rouker A.L
Randle Rouley Y.L
Randle Rouley G.L
John de Rouley Y.L

John de Scolehale A.L
William Sherd G.L
David Shocklach A.L
John Shrigley A.L
John de Southworth G.P
Thomas Spark G.L
Hugh Stevenard A.L
Robert de Sutton G.L

The following have the marginal note *Sagittarius de Corona*:

William Bailiour
Richard le Bailly
John Baker
Robert Barneby
Roger de Barnescawe
William de Barwe

Robert del Halle
William Halowin
David Hampton

Rchard Hampton
Richard de Hankelow
Thomas 1e Harper
Robert 1e Harper
William Haselhurst
William son of Adam de Hatton
Thomas Haynson
Robert de1 Helde
Thomas dei Helde
William de Helegh of Flint
William de Henelegh G.L
Hugh le Hester
John de Herton
Richard de Heiegh sen.
Roger de Holes
Peter del Holt
William Horton
David de Horton
Robert del Hough
Thomas del Hough sen.
Thomas Howe
John Hugge
Hugh de Hulton
Hugh Hunt
Thomas de Huxley
William de Huxley

Robert Kyng

David de Larketon
Patrick de Larketon
Thomas Leche
John de Legh
William de Lea
John son of John Legh de Bagueley
Willlam son of Geoffrey Legh
Robert de Leper
Richard Lightfoote
Thomas Littleover

Randol Minwaring
David de Malpas
John de Marple
John Massey
William Massey
John Massey of Hale
William brother of John Massey of Hale
William de Mostyn
Matthew de Motlorve
Roger de Mottram
Robert de Motlowe

Wiliiam de Overton

Richard de Page
Robert Parker
Thomas Paver
Thomas de Pevere
Thomas Peyntour
Simon Pickering
Robert Pievere
Edmund de Pynyngton
Richard Plat

Matthew de Ratclif
Wiliiam Rayne
Ralph Rede
John Richardson of Thornton
John Roger

Thomas Sand
John de Saughall
William son of John de Saughall
William son of John de Saughall
William Scrivenor
Edmund Sherd
Robert Sherd
Richard de Siddington
Thomas Sidebotham
Thomas Sidnall
Thomas Sidnall

Ralph de Somerford
John de Somerford
Ralph de Somerford de Congleton
Thomas son of Ralph de Somerford
John Somerville
Robert Spark
Robert de Stanley
Nicholas Stoke
William son of Robert Stoke
Randol Stoke
Thomas de Swettenham de Mobberley

William de Tabley
Thomas de Tatton
Robert de Taverner
John Tawer
John Taillour de Thornton
Thomas le Taillour
Thomas Thornteley
Henry de Thornton
John de Tymperlegh
Humphrey de Tyttelegh

William Underwood
Wlliam de Venables
Nicholas le Vemon
William le Vernon
Richard le Vernon

John Waleron
Thomas Walker
Robert son of Wiliiam de Warburton de Neucroft
William de Warburton
Richard de Wereburton
William le Ward de Horton
John de Wardle
John de Wamlingham
Richard son of Ralph de Wever
Richard de Wever de Bowden
Thomas de Westbe
William de Westbe

Robert de Whitley
Howell de Whitney
William de Wiglond. Jun.
Willlam Willet
Richard Wolle de Church Lawton
Stephen del Wode
William Wode
William del Wode. vacheman
David de Wodehouse
Nicholas de Worsley
Robert de Worth
John de Wronou

Robert del Yate de Congleton.

APPENDIX SEVEN

The names of those who served in the various 'watches' of King Richard's bodyguard and their captains.

RALPH DAVENPORT'S WATCH

William Wyot
Robert de Chedle
Richard de Rode
Ranulph Rouley
Robert de Worth
Robert de Harper
John Merpul
William de Huxley
Hugh le Hunt
Walter Wasshynton
Ranulph Denys
John Wyther
Richard Derpley
Thomas Arnecok
Pobert Pyk
William Lytlure
Hugh de Mylyngton
John de Barynton
Hugh Hopkynson
Edmund de Pynyngton
William de Henyley
Hugh de Thorneycoroft
Roger Page
Thomas de Hogh
Henry de Chaderton
Robert Barneby
Hugh de Yekeheth
John Willesfull
Peter Goldesone
Thomas le Smyth
Hugh de Acton
William de Clutton
Howell de Whitney

Robert de Sutton
Hugh de Barton
Humphrey de Tytteley
John Roger
Richard de Neuton
Robert de Motlowe
John Walron
John del Bothe
Thomas de Davenport
Thomas de Betcheton

JOHN DE LEGH'S WATCH

William de Legh
Richard de Helegh
William Baret
William del Sherd
Richard de Helegh, senr.
William de Haselhurst
Gilbert del Twys
Thomas de Henshagh
John Walkeden
Stephen le Lene
Robert Coterell
Roger Mottram
Roger Starkey
Ralph Willaboy
John Couper
Richard de Davenport
Robert le Walker
John de Medewall
Thomas de Workesley
Geoffrey de Workesley
Nicholas de Workesley
Roger de Hawardyn
Robert de Sherd
Edmund del Sherd
John Broumwynd
Richard Cam
John Grymesdyche
William Grymesdyche
John Ins

Adam Arlendes
William Baker
John Duncan
William Chambre
Richard de Ledbeter
William de Ledbeter
Ranulph de Swettenham
Richard del Bradeford
John Cans
Robert del Brugge
John Laurence
John Somerford
Roger de Birkenhed
William de Boydell
John, son of John de Legh de Bayglee, alias John de Legh de Wythenshagh

Richard de Chelmundelegh's Watch

Thomas del Grene
Richard de Rydley
Thomas de Cholmeley
John de Tatton
Henry Walker
Richard Belewe
John Stoteville
John de Golburn de Bunbury
Morgan Ffylkyn
Hugh de Bulkeley
William de Wyglond, senr
David Shocklache
David Hampton
Thomas Hardyng
Richard de Twemlowe
John Blakenhale
Thomas de Pevere
Philip de Rosumgrene
William de Horton
David Dod
Hugh Byrd
William de Wyglond, junr
William le Warde de Horton
John de Salghall

William de Eggesley
Hugh de Bykerton
Thomas de Huxley
David de Larketon
Thomas de Coneway
Owen de Caurden
David de Caurden
Patrick de Larketon
John Wevere
Robert le Taverner
Richard de Cholmeley
Hugh de Cholmeley
Richard de Hampton
Richard de Frodesham
John Broke
John de Horton
Richard Stevenard
Richard Gryfitson
William Tatenall
Eamon de Eton
David de Malpas

Adam de Bostok's Watch

Thomas son of William de Bostok de Bostok
John son of William de Bostok
Thomas son of John de Bostok
John son of David de Bostok
William de Bostok
Thomas son of Adam de Bostok
Thomas de Assheton
John de Crumbewell
Richard son of Ralph de Wevere
Thomas Peyntour
William Warde
John de Kekwyk
William Wych
Thomas Harpoure
John Bouker
Thomas Heth
William de Werberton
Henry de Wetenhale
Laurence de Bentylegh

Henry de Thornton
Robert de Hassall
Thomas Hayneson
John de Dyseworth
John son of John de Wetenhale
Laurence de Bradshagh
Hugh de Hulton
Henry de Pynygton
Thomas Balle
Robert de Pevere
Richard de Lauton
Thomas de Litlure
Richard de Brige
William Huyme
Robert de Sondbache
Roger de Croxton
William de Croxton
William Underwode
Thomas de Sydenhall
Robert Parker
Richard Page
John le Ffyssher
Ranulph de Stoke
Roger de Berneshagh

THOMAS DE BESTON'S WATCH

John Baker
Robert Brescy
John de Wynyngton
Hugh le Smyth
Hugh le Draper
Nicholas Stoke
John Barton
William Glaskerion
William de Hallum
Nicholas Danyel
Roger de Bradford
Richard de Bulkylegh
Roger le Hurtor
John de Wetenhale
William Brayn
David Brayn, senr

David Brayn, jur.
Henry son of David Brayn
Thomas Brayn
Thomas de Hulgrave
John de Dokynton
Thomas Rouland
Thomas Davy
David Seitpierre
Roger Waldene
John Northwode
Richard Plat
John Botham
Henry Hondekynsone Brayn
Thomas de Haselyngton
Thomas Willaboy
John Teynteth
John de Aldresey
John Wermyncham
William de Helegh
David de Horton
Roger de Beston
Thomas de Thornteley
Thomas Tatton
John Hogge
Richard de Honkelowe
Ranulph de Lauton
Henry son of Thomas Brayn
William de Stoke
Hugh de Honster
William de Aldresey

THOMAS DE HOLFORD'S WATCH

William Kyncy
Thomas Kyncy
Robert Kyncy
Robert Wibbe
William Deye
Thomas de Eddesley
John Macy de Hale
John le Mason
Robert de Anderton
William de Tabbeley

Thomas de Bradeshagh
William Rawne
John Prestclyft
Thomas le Mascy
Richard de Wevere
Thomas de Holde
Richard Lytfoot
William Moston
Thomas Spark
Hugh Davy
John de Aynesworth
Thomas Sydebotham
Robert del Hogh
Alexander de Coton
Robert Denys
Ranulph Barett
David de Bostok
William de Berkeswell
Richard Bradford
John son of William le Macy
Ranulph Maynwaring
Roger de Bromley
Adam Denys
John de Wynyngton
Thomas de Mylyngton
John de Sotheworth
Robert Wilme
Hugh le Vernon
Hugh Glayve
David de Alpram
William Fforest

JOHN DONE'S WATCH

Roger Holes
Robert de Stanley
John Donne de Warton
Richard Donne de Warton
William Donne de Kelsale
Richard Donne, brother of William
Richard Wode
William son of Peter Starky
Thomas le Pavere

Robert de Teverton
William Wronowe
William de Grafton
William Fferrour
Ralph Rede
Simon de Hatton
William Hatton
Robert Colswaynesoke
Thomas de Burwes
Peter del Holt
John le Mascy de Kelsale
Thomas Heynesone de Overe
Richard de Assheton
John Tawer
Matthew de Radclyf
Richard de Werberton
Robert de Werberton
William de Barton
William de Overton
John del Clogh
John Ffysh
Richard Bayly
John Bate
Richard Coterell
Thomas Welde
John de Acton
Robert de Craven
Robert Spark
John Wylknsone
Richard Benet
Thomas Leche
John Blumhull
Richard Grene

APPENDIX EIGHT

Between October 1397 and July 1398, a number of Cheshire men received annuities for life or during the King's pleasure, either to retain the men to the King's service or to reward new recruits. The sums granted vary from 100s (£5) to £10, or between ten (£6 13s 4d) to twenty marks (£13 6s 8d). Unless otherwise shown the awards were for life: a 'P' indicates those granted during the King's pleasure. Unless otherwise stated the amount paid is 100s

Some of the applications for recruitment give details of the applicants previous military service, *e.g.* John de Hulgreave, armiger, stated that he had been "in the army for twenty-two years, and at Berwick, in the service of Henry Percy".

John son of Hugh d'Ardeme
Hamo de Ashlee
Lawrence de Aston
John de Audlyme, armiger..........................£20
Robert Ashton
William Beeston
John son of William Beeston
William de Belewe
John Boydell, armiger......................................P
Adam de Bostock
David de Bostock de Churton
Richard de Bostock, armiger
Nicholas de Bradshagh....................................P
William son of William de Brereton
Thomas son of William de Brereton
Richard de Bromlegh ....£10 P
Roger Bruen
Richard Bruen
Nicholas Bulkeley
Nicholas Bulkeley, armiger..........................10 marks
Peter de Bulkeley of Halghton.............................P
George Carrington
Randle Carrington..P
Richard Cholate..P
Hugh Cotton

Hugh Cotton, armiger................................10 marks
William Crue
David son of Thomas Crue de Pulcroft
Thomas de Croke...10 marks
Roger Condeliffe...20 marks
Hugh Cotton, armiger................................£11 13s 4d
Richard le Chelmeslvyk...............................40 marks
William Daniel de Daresbury
William Daniel, armiger
Richard son of Ralph de Davenport, knight
Arthur Davenport
Ralph Davenport...£20
Henry Davenport...P
John Domville de Lymme
John Done..£10
Richard Done..10 marks
William Done de Wharton, armiger..............P
Richard del Dounes
Peter de Dutton, armiger.............................40 marks
Phillip de Egerton
David de Egerton
Ralph de Egerton
Ralph de Egerton, jun.
John de Eton
Vivian de Foxwist
Nicholas de Foxwist
Gilbert Glegge
Robert Griffin, esquire....................................P
John de Hallum, armiger
Gilbert de Halsale, knight..........................£20
Thomas de Halton, armiger......................£10
John de Handforth
John Harding de Twemlow
John de Helegh de Flint
John Hope, clerk to the exchequer of Chester... £10
John de Hulgreave, armiger
Ughtred de Huxley
Hugh de Knottesford.................................20s.
John de Kingsley, armiger..........................20 marks
John de Lathom, esquire.................................P
Robert de Legh, knight..............................40 marks

John de Lea
William de Legh.......................................20 marks
Hugh de Legh
John de Legh de Booths
John de Legh de Macclesfield
Peter de Legh
John son of John de Legh, Kt........................P
Geoffrey son of John de Legh Kt.
John de Litherland
John Littleone
David de Malpas
Richard de Manley
John Mascy of Tatton................................20 marks
Thomas son of John Mascy of Tatton
Roger Mascy of Sale
Robert Mascy of Hale
Richard Mascy of Pudington..................£10 P
Robert Mascy, knight.................................£10 P
William Mascy, esquire...................................P
William de Molyns, knight........................£10
William de Mulneton, esquire
Richard de Nedeham armiger
Thomas Pygot
John de Poole, knight
James de Poole
Ralph de Radclif, knight...........................£40
Richard Redeman.......................................40 marks
Thomas St. Pierre, esquire...............................P
William de Siddington
Robert de Smethwick
Thomas de Somerford
Henry de Spurstow
John de Stanley, knight...............................40 marks
William de Stanley, junr.
John de Sutton, esquire...................................P
Matthew de Swettenham
Henry de Tildeslegh..................................£20
Robert de Toft
William Trafford
Richard de Venables, knight........................20 marks
Richard de Vernon

Thomas de Weever
John de Weever...P
Thomas de Wettenhall de Alpraham............... P
John de Whalley
Peter de Wilbraham
John Williamson de Pulford........................20s.
Richard de Winnington, knight..................20 marks
Thomas de Worth

To Henry de Knottesford's grant of twenty shillings per annum, a further six pence a day was added.

Johl de Helegh's grant was to be paid out of the perquisites of the Court of Flint from 24 July 1397, the following day he was appointed Steward of the court of Flint.

APPENDIX NINE

A list of miscellaneous wages of six, four, three and two pence a day, granted to the men of Cheshire during King Richard's reign.

Lawrence de Aston, 6d., a day for life.
Thomas Bagulegh de Knottesford, senior, 6d. a day for life, having petitioned the King that he had been at Calais with the King's father and at the battle of Poitiers, and elsewhere andnever received any reward.
Adam Bordhewer, armiger, 6d., a day for life.
John Carve, a grant of the office of armourer to all castles of Chester and North Wales with 6d., a day for life.
David Brayn, senior, 6d., a day for life.
William Rotour, armiger, 6d., a day for life.
Richard Rotour, armiger, 6d., a day for life.
Thomas de Wereburton de Aketon, armiger, 6d., a day for life, in recognition of his past services to the King and the King's father, having been taken prisoner five times and wounded.
William de Wettenhall de Alpraham, armiger, a grant of 6d., a day for life.
William son of Anky de Appleton, 4d., a day for life.
Nicholas Brok, 4d., a day for life in consideration for the great travail and labours in the King's wars.
John Brownwynd, 4d., a day for life.
Roger Croxton, 4d., a day for life.
Richard Daniel, 4d., a day for life.
John Dawne de Wharton, 4d., a day for life.
Richard Dawne, brother of John, 4d., a day for life.
Thomas Done, an archer of the Duchy of Chester, 4d., a day for life.
William Done, archer of the Duchy of Chester, 4d., a day for life.
Richard del Grene, archer, 4d., a day for life.
Thomas de Hallum, 4d., a day for life.
Robert de Holes, a grant of 4d., a day for life.
Peter del Ho1te, yeoman of the principality of Chester, 4d., a day for life.
John Hunt de Stopport, 4d., a day for life.
John de Lea de Troghford, esquire, 4d.. a day for life.
Thomas de Venables, esquire, 4d., a day during pleasure.
Tichard de Wodehouse, 4d., a day for life.
Thomas de Wodehouse, 4d., a day for life.

Richard Bruen, 3d., a day for life.
Thomas Bull, 3d., a day for life.
Phillip de Burwes, 3d., a day for life in compensation for great labours in Spain, France and Scotland.
William de Denhall, 3d., a day for life.
Richard de Grenock, 3d., a day for life.
Thomas Hamelet, 3d.. a day for life.
Richard Hampton, 3d., a day for life.
Hankyn de Halton, 3d., a day for life.
William son of Geoffrey Mascy, 3d., a day for life.
Mathew de Radeclif, an archer of the Principality of Chester, 3d., a day for life.
Roger 1e Taillour, 3d., a day for life.
Roger Denys, 3d., a day for life.
Richard de Doddington, servant to the Duke of Exeter, 3d., a day for life on being appointed park keeper at Eyton, Wales.
Warren Edwardsone de Altringham, 2d.,a day for life.
Henry Ferror, 2d., a day for life.
Henry Gervys, 2d., a day for life.
Richard Harding, 2d., a day for life.
Richard Mason, 2d., a day for life.
Henry Mascy,2d., a day for life.
Thomas Nelde, 2d., a day for life.
John Newburgh, 2d., a day for life.
Hugh Pickering,2d., a day for life.
Edmund de Pynyngton ,2d., a day for life.
Phillipe de Sondebache, 2d., a day for life for services in Spain, Guinne and elsewhere and of his wound sustained whilst bailiff of the principality of Chester.
Edward Sherd, 2d., a day for life.
John de Twembrokes, 2d., a day for life.
Simon de Twys, 2d., a day for life.
Thomas Williamson de Bostok, 2d., a day for life.
John Williamson de Bostok, 2d., a day for life.
John Lawless, a grant of 26s. 8d., per annum, in consideration of his good service in wars and having lost his eyesight in the same.
Howell de Eton, serjeant-at-arms, 12d., a day during pleasure.
John Norreys, serjeant-at-arms, 12d., a day for life.
Hamo Smethwick, on being appointed one of the thirty serjeants-at-arms to the King, 12d., a day for life.
Nicholas d'Orrell, 12d., a day, following a petition stating that he had

been in the King's service for many years in France, Ireland and Scotland; also at sea with Sir John d'Arundell, at Radcote Brugge, at Garghwell in Ireland, and afterward *sen v're hon'able s'vice et le s'de Beaumont en Kenslee* in Ireland, and has lost three hundred marks.

APPENDIX TEN

Miscellaneous grants of offices, pardons, etc., granted throughout Richard II reign.

Richard de Aston, Kt., commissioned to arrest disturbers of the peace in 1392.
Henry de Birtles, appointed Justice of Chester in 1391.
Henry Brayn, appointed to arrest disturbers of the peace, in Nantwich Hundred, 1386.
Henry de Birtles appointed sergeant at law in Chester and Flint, 1399.
William de Brereton,Kt., commission to arrest disturbers of the peace in Northwich Hundred, 1386.
William de Brereton, commission to levy a subsidy, 1391.
William de Brereton, commission to arrest evil doers, 1390.
William de Brereton, commission to arrest disturbers in Broxton, 1392.
John Brickhull, a yeoman of the chamber of the Duke of Ireland, a grant of the mill of Adecrosse and the profits therefrom, during pleasure, 1391.
Henry de Beeston, commission to arrest disturbers, 1391.
Hugh Browe, commission to raise archers, 1391.
Robert de Carrington, a grant of a pardon, on account of his great labours in service to the King, as also for the great love and affection which the King has for his lieges of Chester, which he lately named his Principality, 1398.
Thomas Cholmondeley, a grant of the custody and profits of the bridge at Holt, 1398.
John Cranmere, appointed a yeoman of the King's wardrobe, 1398.
Janekyn de Crue, appointed park keeper at Ruyton for life, 1397.
Richard Crouther de Middlewich, yeoman, archer of the Principality of Wales, a grant of letters of enfranchisement of the town of Middlewich, 1397.
Edward Carrington, commission to arrest disturbers, 1392.
Robert Daniel of Rydelegh and Richard Cholmondeley, commission to arrest disturbers, 1386.
Thomas de Davenport de Bechton (as Daniel above).
Thomas de Davenport, appointed Justice of Chester, 1388.
John Delves, commission to arrest John Mascy of Tatton and Thomas Talbot. kt., and convey each to Chester Castle, 1393.

Laurence de Dutton, commission to arrest disturbers in Bucklow, 1392
Thomas Dawne, appointed park keeper at Bramhurst, Oswestry, for life, 1398.
Peter de Dutton, appointed Constable of Chirk, during pleasure, 1391.
Peter de Dutton, commission to raise archers, 1399.
Phillip de Egerton, commission to raise archers, 1398.
John de Eton. commission to raise archers, 1399.
Laurence Fitton, commission to raise archers, 1399.
Thomas Fouleshurst, commission to raise archers, 1399.
Nicholas Foxwist, armiger, appointed Steward of Hawarden, during pleasure, 1391.
Vivian Foxwist and John de Tyldeslegh to arrest malefactors in Wirral, 1386.
John Golofre Kt., appointed sheriff of Flint for life, also Constable and Raglot of Flint, 1390.
Robert de Grosvenor, commissioned to arrest disturbers, 1386.
Nicholas Hauberk, Kt., to succeed Golofre, deceased, 1396.
William del Holte, commissioned to arrest disturbers, 1385.
John de Haukestone, commissioned to raise archers, 1398.
William de Helegh, appointed as park keeper at Shotwick, 1397.
Geoffrey de Knyerton, 'un de noz archiers' appointed park keeper of Glynthewdok for life, 1397.
John de Legh Kt., appointed constable of Oswestry for life with £10 p.a., 1397.
Hugh de Legh de Legh, appointed Escheator of the Principality of Chester during pleasure, 1397.
William de Legh, commissioned to raise archers.
John Mascy of Putington Kt., Hamo Mascy and others, commissioned to take ships and seamen that they find between Holyhead and Furness, to convey them Chester for the transport of Roger Mortimer and his retinue, 1397.
John Mascy of Puddington Kt., appointed Vice-justice of Chester, 1396.
John Mascy of Tatton Kt. Appointed Sheriff of Chester, 1389.
John Mascy of Puddington Kt.. appointed steward of Harwarden, 1397.
John Leche, a pardon for good service, 1384.
William de Tabley, appointed bailiff of Bucklow, 1389.

Thomas de Tatton a grant of the clerkship of Bromfeld and Yale during pleasure, 1391.

APPENDIX ELEVEN

"The names of the knights and esquires of the County of Chester who had the officering and leading of five hundred archers of the said county towards Scotland in the month of July in the first year of the reign of Henry the fourth."

MACCLESFIELD HUNDRED

Robert de Legh, Chivaler
Ralph de Davenport
William de Assheton
Reginald del Dounes ....thirty-six archer

John son of Hugh d'Arderne
Robert de Davenport
John de Honford de Honford
Nicholas de Davenport..............thirty-four archers

William de Venables de Bolyn
Laurence Fyton.......................twenty-four archers

Thomas de Worth....................six archers

BUCKLOW HUNDRED

John de Mascy of Tatton
Thomas de Mascy, his son.........twenty-four archers

William de Legh, chivaler
John Savage...........................twenty-five archers

Peter Dutton..........................twelve archers
John de Holford
Robert de Toft........................twelve archers

Ralph de Legh
John Doumvill de Lyme...........eight archers

Thomas Danyers
George de Caryngton...............twelve archers
Hugh de Legh
Robert de Assheton..................ten archers

NORTHWICH HUNDRED

Richard de Venables, chivaler
William de Brereton.................twenty archers

Thomas le Grosvenor
Ralph le Maynwaryng...............sixteen archers

Adam de Bostok
John de Whelock.....................sixteen archers

William de Holt, junior
John Harding of Twemlow.........eight archers

BROXTON HUNDRED

Richard Cholmondelegh...........twenty archers
John Brid
Ralph de Eggerton....................ten archers

John de Elton
William le Belewe...........................ten archers
instead of David de Bostok who is ill.

William de Mulneton, junior
John del Lee........................... ten archers

David de Eggerton....................ten archers

NANTWICH HUNDRED

Richard de Vernon....................twenty archers

Richard de Mascy del Hough
Thomas 1e Maistresonne.............ten archers

Thomas le Vernon
John de Kyngeslegh ....ten archers

Roger de Mascy del Hogh
William de Crue de Sonde...........ten archers

Peter de Munshull
Nicholas de Bulkelegh............... ten archers

Eddisbury Hundred

Richard de Wynyngton. chivaler
John de Wynyngton, his son ....twenty archers

Thomas de Bromley
Wiliiam le Rotour......................fifteen archers

Thomas de Beston
Roger le Bruyn........................ fifteen archers

Hugh de Dutton
Willlam de Venables de Troghford...fifteen archers

OTHER BOOKS BY TONY BOSTOCK

CHESHIRE'S MONUMENTS TO THE PAST: PART 1. MEDIEVAL EFFIGIES

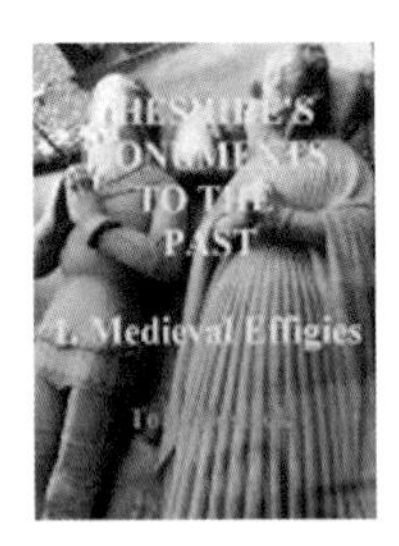

TODAY, UNDERSTANDABLY, many of our churches remain closed to those who wish to seek peace and solitude and a place in which to contemplate and pray. Locked also to the casual visitor, tourist or student who may wish to view their treasures which form part of our heritage. This book is the first of two which lists lists and records Cheshire monuments to be found in the various churches dating from the Medieval period: that is before the 1530s. This ebook is a straight-forward source of reference to these sepruchal monuments with details of where they may be found, their dates, styles of armour or costume and something of the persons antecedents and family. It should appeal to all have an interest in Cheshire history as well as anyone having an general interest in historical costume. ISBN 978-0-9956857-2-7

CHESHIRE'S MONUMENTS TO THE PAST: PART 2. TUDOR & STUART EFFIGIES

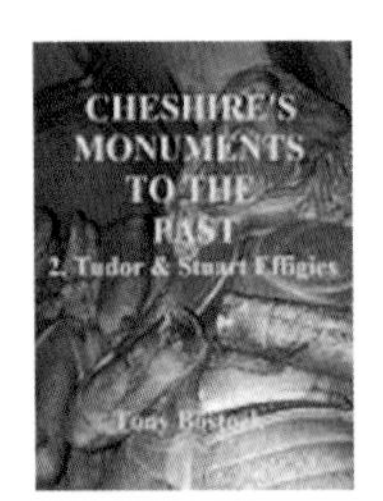

THIS BOOK is the second of two which lists lists and records Cheshire monuments to be found in the various churches dating from the Tudor and Stuart periods: that is after the 1530s.
This ebook is a straight-forward source of reference to these sepruchal monuments with details of where they may be found, their dates, styles of armour or costume and something of the persons antecedents and family. It should appeal to all have an interest in Cheshire history as well as anyone having an general interest in historical costume.
ISBN 978-0-9956857-3-4

Dogs of War

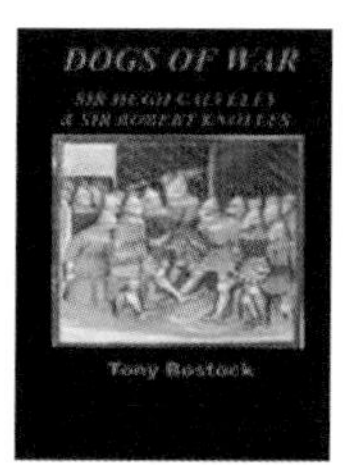

TWO OF THE GREATEST HEROES of the Hundred Years Wars, arguably nationally and certainly so far as Cheshire is concerned, were Sir Hugh Calveley and Sir Robert Knolles. In addition to their military prowess, these men, who seem to have been closely related, are remarkable as being examples of social mobility. Both came from humble backgrounds, perhaps Knolles being the more so, and yet they managed to rise to high positions in 14th century England – Knolles even commanding the English forces on a campaign into France, a position normally reserved for those of royal or at least ducal status. Their military prowess and leadership earned them legendary status within their own time so that many contemporary chroniclers recorded their adventures and exploits. This book will detail their respective lives which were inextricably linked.

ISBN 978-0-9956857-1-0

Bostock: A History of a Cheshire Village and its People

TODAY'S BOSTOCK is a relatively young village in comparison with the original Saxon settlement of 'Botestoch' noted in the Doomsday Book of 1086. Its residents have fought for their country from Agincourt to the second World War, and it has seen agriculture move from oxen pulling ploughs to the very latest hi-tech machinery. The neat black and white cottages which now stand in the village were built as recently as 1775, but the village's origins lie at least 700 years earlier, probably before William the Conqueror's victory at the Battle of Hastings in 1066.

As a noted Conservation Area, Bostock is probably one of the most perfectly preserved villages in the county, and can trace its history through the various wealthy families who at one time owned over 30,000 acres of land. Through these families there are important

connections with world trade, literary figures and eminent architects and landscapers.
The original publication of *BOSTOCK: A History of a Village and its people* (2009) rapidly sold out and since then there have been many requests for copies by many people from various places in the UK and abroad. Producing the book in this format allows many people to access it and hopefully enjoy the information they can take from reading it. ISBN 978-0-9956857-4-1

WINSFORD: A HISTORY OF A CHESHIRE TOWN AND ITS PEOPLE

WINSFORD HAS AN UNUSUAL dual identity, being the amalgamation in 1894 of the ancient townships of Wharton on the east of the River Weaver and Over on the west, to create a Victorian 'new town'. Both are mentioned in the pages of the Domesday Book, and the Cistercian abbey and convent of Vale Royal dominated the history of Over. Though originally in an area of predominantly pastoral farming, the district around Winsford owed its prosperity to the extraction of salt from the rock salt beds that lie beneath much of mid-Cheshire. From the late 17th century, brine was extracted and evaporated to produce salt, and from 1844 salt was also obtaining by mining.
Today Winsford is a town in the very heart of Cheshire. It is best known perhaps as the home of a car supermarket that bears an appropriate name, and also as home to the rock salt mines whose product is spread on our nation's roads to combat the perils of ice and snow. Historically Winsford is a relatively new town, having been performed in 1894 when the Winsford Urban District Council was established. Published by Leonie Press.
ISBN 978-1-909727-22-9

Owners, Occupiers and Others: Seventeenth Century Northwich

Northwich in the 17th century was a small market town of about six acres, concentrated on a plot of low-lying flat land at the confluence of the rivers Dane and Weaver, and surrounded by fields and meadows on the slopes of the neighbouring townships. Lying in the very heart of the county of Cheshire, it was a significant transport hub and trading centre.

It had been an important salt-making site since Roman times and could be described as an industrial town in a pre-industrial age. The raw material - high quality brine - came from a pit on the banks of the Dane and was channelled along wooden troughs to 108 wich-houses where it was boiled in lead pans to extract the salt. The proprietors and entrepreneurs involved were subject to time-honoured complex rules that regulated when, where and how the salt could be made. The 17th century was a particularly interesting period of history - an era of social, economic, political and religious change that affected the lives of every individual in some way. Plague, fires, flooding and the Civil War all left their mark on the town and its inhabitants.

To assist genealogists and local historians the book has been comprehensively indexed. The index can be consulted on-line at Leonie Press, so that you can see if there is mention of a person, place or event of interest to you.

Published by Leonie Press. ISBN 978-1-901253-37-5

NOT AVAILABLE AS AN E-BOOK

Printed in Poland
by Amazon Fulfillment
Poland Sp. z o.o., Wrocław

80930326R00109